Praise for *I Wish My Dad: The Power of Vulnerable Conversations between Fathers and Sons*

"As a father and the product of a fatherless home, I can say: this book is gold. We need tools, roadmaps, and sage wisdom to become who we were made to be and reinvest in the next generation. The heartfelt transparency of the stories in *I Wish My Dad* gives men permission to share their truth, heal, and learn the emotional skills needed for healthy father-and-son relationships."

—**LeCrae**, Grammy Award–winning hip-hop artist and *New York Times* bestselling author

"Healthy and vulnerable spaces for men and their sons are a necessity in today's culture. The stories shared by fathers and sons in *I Wish My Dad* allow readers a glimpse into the emotional needs of men that few rarely get to express. This book shares truths that need to be heard."

—**David Michael Wyatt**, singer and songwriter

"*I Wish My Dad* serves as the model for men to have conversations, leading to healing and strengthening of father-and-son relationships that will have a positive impact for generations."

—**Nicole L. Cammack**, PhD, licensed clinical psychologist, and president and CEO of Black Mental Wellness

"Romal Tune's authenticity and genuine desire to be a better father, combined with the strength and courage of his son, gives us a powerful, honest, humble, and hopeful invitation to become better together through honesty, openness, and love. The stories shared by men in this book will change your life and your relationships."

—**Danielle Strickland**, author, speaker, and advocate

"Vulnerability is a contagious cure. Tune models that with every page in this book. *I Wish My Dad* has the potential to cure us from our despair and free us to hope again."

—**John Onwuchekwa**, pastor of Cornerstone Church and cofounder of Portrait Coffee

"*I Wish My Dad* is more than a right-on-time read; it is an invitation for fathers and sons to be the curators of the change they are seeking to see in themselves and in their families. The stories in this love-offering of a book will help to heal hearts, homes, and relationships between fathers and sons."

—**Shawn Dove**, founder of Corporation for Black Male Achievement and managing partner of New Profit

"*I Wish My Dad* is emotional, insightful, humbling, palatable, challenging, and needed; you will come away not only rooting for these men, but believing there is hope for yourself."

—**A. D. "Lumkile" Thomason**, author and filmmaker

"Romal and Jordan masterfully invite us not only into the struggles of father-and-son relationships, but they give a voice to the endless possibilities that can heal those broken relationships. *I Wish My Dad* shines a light on the art of listening and the hope we have when we truly hear each other."

—**Preston Perry**, poet, teacher, and apologist

"Hearing these men's stories has given me access to the conversations my father and I have yet to share. I am more tender, more compassionate now toward my father. There is healing within these pages for sons no doubt, and daughters as well."

—**Juanita Rasmus**, author of *Learning to Be: Finding Your Center after the Bottom Falls Out*

I WISH MY DAD

I WISH MY DAD

THE POWER OF VULNERABLE CONVERSATIONS BETWEEN FATHERS AND SONS

ROMAL TUNE
WITH JORDAN TUNE

BROADLEAF BOOKS
MINNEAPOLIS

Cover photo: Sheretta Danielle Photography
Cover design: 1517 Media

Print ISBN: 978-1-5064-8157-9
eBook ISBN: 978-1-5064-8158-6

"I have felt for my father a longing that was almost physical, something passionate … It has bewildered me, even thrown me into depression. It is mysterious to me exactly what it is I wanted from my father. I have seen this longing in other men—and see it now in my own sons, their longing for me. I think that I have glimpsed it once or twice in my father's feelings about his father. What surprises me is how angry a man becomes sometimes in the grip of what is, in essence, an unrequited passion."

—Lance Morrow, *The Chief*

"If trauma can be passed down through generations, then so can healing."

—Matthew Williams

CONTENTS

CONTENTS

A FATHER'S INTRODUCTION

ROMAL TUNE
(JORDAN'S FATHER)

I did not grow up with my dad. He had a relationship with my mother for a time, but when they broke up, he vanished. I never knew why they didn't make it; neither he nor my mother shared many details. I heard snippets here and there, but the full story never came together.

I was raised in California, by my mom, along with the help of my grandparents. My mom and I moved frequently—sometimes because we didn't have money and sometimes because my mom felt a neighborhood was too dangerous. As a result, I attended a different school every year from elementary up until the eleventh grade, when I met my dad.

Before I met my dad, I had the worst thoughts about him, including wishing he were dead. As much as I tried to ignore his existence, I couldn't. The disdain grew as I got older, and it festered in me. So when I first met my father when I was fifteen years old, it was awkward—for both of us. I had developed a personality and habits shaped by the struggles of growing up in poverty and being surrounded by crime and addiction. Survival was all I knew. My dad hadn't been there to protect me from dangers or to help me understand what it means to be a good man.

1

A year after meeting him, I moved in with him, his wife, and their three sons for two years. They lived in a world I had only seen on television: a spacious home with a white picket fence in the suburbs of New Jersey, while I had been moving from place to place with my mom just trying to survive. Once I moved there, however, our true personalities emerged and often clashed. I detested the idea of chores. He drank too much. I skipped school. He had a volatile temper. I rebelled. He cursed at me. I consorted with the wrong crowd. He got angrier. In the end, after two years of conflict, I moved in with my grandparents before heading off to basic training and the army. My relationship with my father returned to what it had been before that time: nothing.

For the next fifteen years we were estranged, a period of time in which the original feelings of abandonment, confusion, disappointment, and anger reemerged. I was not paralyzed by my father's absence—I went on with my life. But I was, in a way, haunted by it. I served in the army for four years, and then became a student at Howard University. A year after graduating from Howard, I attended Duke University School of Divinity. Both of my children, Aman and Jordan, were born during that time.

Finally, in 2017, my father and I reconnected. I visited him in Houston, where he had moved. It was a pleasant, encouraging time together. We had grown in different ways, and we were now able to communicate with each other with civility and as men. Our time together was so fulfilling that I left that visit with a thought: *I wish my dad had spent more time with me.*

I wish my dad ... That sentence fragment grabbed my attention, causing me to pause and reflect. I came up with lots of different ways to finish the sentence. Finishing that thought allowed me to give voice to all the things I had longed for from my father. It gave me an outlet for emotions that I didn't even know I had.

I wish my dad ... Finishing the sentence gave me a way to be honest with what I had yearned for, a way to name the love for my father that created those longings in the first place. It was a way to identify what was missing and to admit that I needed things from my dad. Completing that sentence was a way to say that I yearned for deeper connection with my father and that my relationship with him felt incomplete.

You have to diagnose a heart condition before you can find the right prescription. There is medicine for the broken heart of a son, and it involves breaking the silent oath of being "a strong man." It involves naming the pain on the other side of the thought: *I wish my dad . . .*

It was such a simple start to a sentence. But I began to wonder whether it contained the power to heal wounds I didn't even know I had.

The Sentence That Changes Everything

Was I the only man with unfinished business with his dad? Was I the only one who had a broken or sometimes nonexistent relationship with his father? I couldn't be alone in this, I thought. Census data shows that of the 121 million men in the United States, about 60 percent of us are fathers to biological, step, or adopted children. That's a lot of dads. Perhaps other men's wishes about their fathers were not totally unfilled. Or perhaps their wish list was even more extensive than mine.

What if my father had been around when I was growing up? What if he had been the kind of father I needed, giving me guidance and affection? Surely his impact on me would have made me a more emotionally sound person. Surely I would have become a better father myself.

Men are equipped to move on, lower our heads, and do what's necessary to survive and maybe even thrive. Or so we think. But the absence or shortcomings of a father in our lives is always there, playing a role in who we become.

I wanted to hear from other men about their dad wishes and find out if other men longed for things from their fathers that they hadn't received. So I started reaching out to friends and coworkers—men I knew in some capacity and would randomly invite to my home office for conversations about their fathers.

I ended up interviewing dozens of men. Some had good or mostly good relationships with their fathers, and others' relationships with their dads were difficult or simply nonexistent. All but one "I Wish My Dad" interview took place at my home. Some of the men were local, some drove hours to Atlanta, Georgia, where I live, and most flew in from various cities for our conversations. I intentionally selected men of different cultures, ages, and socioeconomic environments. I wanted to see what, if any, common desires for relationships with our fathers transcended differences. Turns out that there are common threads among sons: from those who grew up in poverty—sharecropping and picking cotton—to middle-class men to wealthy aristocrats. Although their environments were different, all the men I interviewed wanted to experience love, affection, and time with their fathers.

After the third interview, I put a box of tissues in my office. At some point while sharing his story, every man cried. As one heartfelt conversation after another unfolded, I received tender, transparent, and emotional stories. Each chapter in this book centers on the story told to me by one of the men I interviewed, who graciously gave me their permission to share their story in this book. (Some names have been changed to protect individuals' privacy.) Some of the stories are tender and demonstrate the loving care of fathers who themselves were wounded but who managed to offer their children what they did not receive themselves. Some of the stories are hard to read and may be especially difficult for readers who have had traumatic experiences.

Many of the "I Wish My Dad" stories in these pages recount adverse childhood experiences (ACEs), which are traumatic events that occur in a child's life between infancy and the age of seventeen. These events can include witnessing intimate partner violence, experiencing chronic poverty, having an incarcerated loved one, witnessing violence in the community, or having a family member die by suicide. This list is not exhaustive. Research shows that all adults have experienced at least one ACE. The more ACEs someone has, the greater the risk they are at for a host of chronic health conditions, mental health vulnerabilities, and substance misuse in adulthood. These stories demonstrate how sons cope with traumatic experiences and either work toward healing or pass trauma on to their own children.

Each chapter gives us a view of the common longings expressed by sons, and also includes a section of takeaways, which my good friend Kyndra Frazier helped to draft. Kyndra was the founding executive director of HOPE Center Harlem, which works to remove barriers to mental health access for communities of color. She is now the CEO of Selah R&R Inc., working to launch a boutique hotel, resort, and conference center focused on intentional rest and holistic health. She has worked as a therapist, and she holds a master of social work degree from Columbia University and a master of divinity degree from Candler School of Theology.

These are sacred stories that stretch beyond generations: of courage, vulnerability, and transparency. The lessons that those of us who are fathers can learn through the stories will be pronounced. Listening to these sons' "I Wish My Dad" stories, we learn to show up emotionally; to meet our kids where they are; to express genuine concern for their feelings and listen without judgment; to create a safe space in our homes where our children feel loved, respected, heard, and valued. We can learn from both the healthy and loving choices these fathers made and from the unhealthy and unloving ones. If a son learns the transformative power of a father's words, the healing touch of a dad's hands, and the critical impact of a dad being fully present, he learns how to be a father and an emotionally healthier man for people in his life. While many of these stories point to the ways fathers fail to give their sons what they need, many also introduce us to fathers living out healthy, loving relationships with their sons.

As I talked with more and more sons about what they had longed for from their fathers, I found that conversation centered on three key areas: love, physical affection, and quality time. Saying "I love you" to other men—even to our sons—and showing them physical affection can be uncomfortable for some men. But I heard sons longing to have heard their dads say "I love you" and to have been hugged by their dads. And I heard them longing to have spent quality time with their dads; in fact, fathers spending time with sons in ways that meet their sons' needs rather than in ways that are convenient and comfortable for fathers emerged as a critical theme.

The men in these conversations did something that many men rarely do: We allowed ourselves to be vulnerable. We passed on the superficial niceties, posturing, and bravado that often create shallow relationships and allowed ourselves to be seen on a deeper level. We embraced words and expressions we knew would pain us. But we did it for a worthwhile reason: healing memories from our childhoods and moving toward reconciling relationships with our fathers.

Over and over men would say things like "I have never thought about this before," or "I've never shared this publicly." I realized, through the course of these conversations, that it is not the case that men don't want to talk about their feelings. We are simply rarely invited to do so.

We live in a world where men are expected to be tough. We are expected to carry heavy burdens without breaking down; it's almost as if the more emotional weight we bear without flinching is some kind of badge of honor, and that crying is a sign of weakness. What I came to realize—and what you will come to realize as you read these stories—is that all men need is permission to be vulnerable and to tell their stories.

Now I see why so many men were eager to tell their stories: they were finally being given permission to be vulnerable in a safe space. If you are a son or a father or both, know that you have permission to feel, to be vulnerable, to cry, and to do whatever it takes to heal. By reading this book, you can set out on a new journey of wholeness that liberates you from unhealthy ideas of manhood that have never served us well.

The stories I heard from other men were so strong and compelling that I began to wonder what would happen if sons started telling their own fathers, directly, what they longed for. What if sons and fathers could talk to each other with the same vulnerability and authenticity that characterized my conversations with men about their fathers?

And beyond that: how could I write a book about men and their sons sharing "I Wish My Dad" stories if I was not willing to go through the experience myself?

Bringing the Conversation Home

I decided to create a space for my son Jordan to share his own "I Wish My Dad" story with me. At the time, my son was attending Morehouse College in Atlanta, and I had been sharing with him about the book for weeks. When I invited Jordan to talk with me about what he wished that I, as his father, had been or done, he responded, "Are you sure you want to do this?"

I think that was his kind way of saying, "You're not going to like what I have to say."

But the difficult conversation had to happen. I wanted us to stop ignoring the strained relationship that hovered between us, and the only way to do that was to address the past head on. If he could speak honestly about what he longed for from me, and if I could listen with a clear heart and open mind? Well, that would be the foundation of building something new and special.

I knew Jordan's feelings would impact me, cut through me, and shame me. But I knew I had to take the harsh truth to get to another place with my son. I did not want Jordan to be burdened with the unexpressed feelings that would not serve him well in life; I knew all too well what that was like. I wanted him to release the baggage that really was not his. It was mine. It was time for him to unload it.

Still, I was restless and did not sleep well the week leading up to my conversation with my son. When it occurred, I listened, asked questions as he shared. I did not respond or attempt to explain anything…although I wanted to. It was not a time for me to speak. It was time for me to listen.

I pushed Jordan to be honest and told him that he didn't have to avoid hurting my feelings. I know who I was back then: I wasn't a good person, and I wanted him to know that it was okay to call it like he saw it. I'm not going to lie. It hurt for me to hear a lot of what he said. But it hurt him even more to have lived through my mistakes as a father. Through that interview, the healing process began. The tension that we carried around for much of our lives dissipated. It was a breaking point—in a good way—for our relationship. Something broke open between us that day. We broke the silence of unspoken truths and climbed the wall that was a barrier to something better and healthier.

Jordan and I are now honest with each other. (You'll find an introduction from Jordan next.) We talk more often. He shares things he deals with in school, with friends, and in dating. He shares his anxieties, fears, doubts, hopes, and dreams with me. It is clear that many of his emotional challenges earlier in life were collateral damage from me, caused by the broken relationship I had with my father. I hadn't dealt with my own stuff, and the scrap metal hit him when things blew up.

The day Jordan shared his "I Wish My Dad" story with me was a gift from God. It was one of the most life-changing and healing things I have ever done. You'll find a partial transcript of that conversation in the resource section at the back of the book. I also wanted my son to have the opportunity to ask questions and hear *my* "I Wish My Dad" story, about my own father, so that is included as well. You'll also find tips for how to have your own "I Wish My Dad" conversation with your father or your son.

A special word here for you if you are a son taking the first steps to build a relationship with your father: Seeking the attention of a man who seemingly has no interest in you is a troublesome road. Those fathers who have not maintained relationships with their sons are usually so burdened with guilt that they find it difficult to take the first step. It is easier for them to live with guilt than face what could be rejection. If you are a son taking the initiative to start or restart a relationship with your father, know that it's not easy but that it's worth the attempt. Offer yourself grace. Be patient and kind to yourself. It took a while to become who you've been, and it will take a while to become the next best version of yourself.

Many of the men I interviewed went on to have their own "I Wish My Dad" conversations with their fathers. A few of the stories you'll read are from men whose dads are no longer living. They will not have the opportunity to have a face-to-face conversation. But I learned that it was still helpful for them to tell the story. They found that giving voice to their feelings and desires was refreshing and that a weight of silence was still lifted.

If you're not able to have an "I Wish My Dad" conversation with your father, you may find it helpful to have that conversation with a therapist who can guide you through it. Perhaps talking to someone who is a father figure to you might help. You may also find journaling to be helpful, as writing can help you release and give voice to what you've been holding inside. Even if your father is no longer living, you can learn from your own stories about what you needed then and what you need now in order to love yourself and others well.

Everyone, not just fathers, can glean something from these "I Wish My Dad" stories. So fathers, as you read these chapters, you surely will encounter some situations, both positive and negative, that seem familiar. Hopefully they will inspire you to change and begin the process of healing with your son. Mothers, you might see bold, relatable issues in these stories that will inspire you to facilitate a coming-together of your son and his father. All of us, including those who aren't parents, might be inspired to prompt an "I Wish My Dad" conversation between a nephew, a cousin, or a friend and his dad.

We can all cultivate or influence healthy, loving father-son relationships among the people we love. My hope is that this book will prompt you to start the conversations.

A SON'S INTRODUCTION

JORDAN TUNE
(ROMAL'S SON)

Feelings can dissipate like smoke in the wind. Or they can linger in your system like an infection that slowly deteriorates your health. I know something about the latter.

My mind and heart have harbored feelings of discontent for my father since he and my mother got divorced when I was seven. I hated him for the way he treated my mother, the way he treated my sister and me, and his less-than-noble actions. As disturbed as I was by all this, I never mustered the courage to confront him about my feelings. I held it in, and as the years passed, we grew apart.

Over time, the fear faded as the emotional distance between us increased. It was not what I wanted. I wanted the type of father I knew he could be—the type of father I had seen before in him. I wanted a father–son relationship driven by love and respect and time spent together. I wanted to learn from my father, to admire him. I wanted him to be so admirable that I would aspire to be like him. Instead, by the time I graduated from high school, we had spent most of my life apart, and we knew very little about each other.

My dad's absence from my life, however, did not quash my desire to succeed. In fact, I didn't realize it at the time, but his lack of connection to me inspired me to achieve. Somewhere in the recesses of my mind, I resented him, and I wanted to show him that I could do it without him. That's the power of fatherhood. It can have a negative or positive influence on your feelings and become the source of motivation (or lack thereof).

As if forces were working to bring us together, we both ended up in Atlanta. My dad had moved there for work a year before I enrolled at Morehouse College, the famed historically Black university. This was my chance to show my dad how much I'd grown and to tell him how I felt. But I was uncertain how to do it. I had fear and anxiety over what I wanted to say and how to say it. I wasn't sure if I could do it.

In what had to be divine intervention, my father told me he was writing a book about what sons really want from their fathers. I did not hesitate to take advantage of the opportunity. He would interview me, and later I would interview him about his relationship with his dad. I was excited to sit down and release all the feelings that I had held in for so long. I was confident that having an open and frank discussion would allow us to have a better relationship—a relationship I could feel good about and, over time, cherish. I needed to move away from the anger that festered in me. This was the time to do it.

As the interview neared, though, my anxiety grew. What if my dad didn't give me the answers I wanted…I needed? Through the years of disconnection and anger, my desire for a genuine father–son relationship had never faded. I wanted this to work out, and I was worried that I would be disappointed.

Listening Led to Healing

The day of our conversation arrived. During the conversation, I asked him about his actions toward me, how he could allow us to grow apart. I told him how his actions made me feel, and I listened carefully to his answers. I sensed regret and sincerity in his voice and words.

Before long, I began to understand what was happening. In that moment, the healing was already starting. The interview itself was one of the most meaningful memories I have with my dad. We were open and honest, and that vulnerability allowed us to create long-lasting solutions for the future. It was like therapy, only better.

I left that conversation with my dad genuinely feeling lighter and free of the emotional baggage that had weighed me down for more than a decade. He helped me understand the root of certain internal issues I've faced since I was young. I am a better person with a clearer mind and heart after facing my dad, sharing my strong feelings, and listening to him without judgment.

This powerful moment in my life will shape the rest of my life. My dad and I have come to a better place, something that, at one point, did not seem possible. But our story illuminates the dynamic virtue of open conversation and the majesty of reconciliation.

By bringing together men to have conversations about their fathers, this book is a significant step to healing for many. For some, it might even help to restore one of life's most significant connections. Broken relationships can be healed, despite discord, distrust, and misunderstandings.

Every son should be able to let his father know how the mistakes he made have negatively impacted his life, how a father's distance or choices have created anger and an unhealthy relationship. And every father should have the opportunity to hear these things: to listen with an open heart, and to learn from the honest interaction. Those two elements—honest sharing, open listening—create something truly special.

My hope is that fathers and sons will use our example as a force to find their way to a better place. Overcoming long-held resentments can be challenging. But the fact that my dad and I are now working on our relationship is a clear example that it can be done.

CHAPTER 1

I WISH MY DAD DIDN'T SILENCE MY VOICE

ERNEST

Whenever Ernest talks about his dad, he lights up with pride and admiration. They had an enviable father-son bond. But Ernest did not feel comfortable enough to verbalize his thoughts to his dad, particular during stressful times. And that has impacted him all of his life.

There is power in being able to speak up, especially in challenging situations. An adult's freedom to express himself is often informed by his childhood experiences and the leeway parents granted—or did not grant—to be vocal.

Encouraging children to verbalize their thoughts leads them to feel comfortable in establishing a presence. But forbidding kids to speak up can stunt their willingness to do so later in life. If a young person's voice is silenced, it can result in regret, dismay, and a hypervigilance to make sure his voice is heard.

Ernest is thirty-five years old, married to Keneta, and lives in northern Virginia. His father did not allow him to freely share his feelings, and his story crystallizes how that hindrance early in life can create adult misgivings. Even if the majority of your childhood is fulfilling, being silenced has lasting effects.

Watching a Father at Work

When Ernest arrives at my home office, it is clear that he is ready to talk about his dad. Sitting across a glass coffee table from me, he leans back in the chair, looks up as if to reflect on fond memories, and smiles. Ernest jumps right in without much prompting. "My father loved being my father," he tells me. "He reveled in it. As a result, I loved being his son and flourished in his love and attention. He made my childhood fun, an adventure that would carry me throughout my life. He had a big personality. Vibrant. Driven. Ambitious."

Ernest's father could connect with most anyone. He treated everyone the same and could have a meaningful conversation with anyone. When he walked into the room, it seemed everyone there was his friend. Ernest tells me that his dad could connect with those who were not as educated or privileged as he was and that he did not project any condescension. He was the same person at work as at home. "He took me practically everywhere with him," Ernest says, adding that he loved going places with his dad. "If he went to the corner store, I went with him. If he went to the governor's mansion or met with the state legislature, he took me with him. On each of those occasions, I was fascinated by how comfortable he was—and how people gravitated to him. I felt proud to be his son."

Ernest's father was a professional educator, a friend, a parent, and a spouse, and he excelled at each role. From one phase of his life to another, he was consistent. He also had the unique ability to blend those different parts of his life seamlessly. So as a child, Ernest often watched his father at work, first as a school principal and then as a superintendent of schools. He saw the way he operated in boardrooms, classrooms, professional settings, and conferences.

Ernest was one of the fortunate sons who grew up knowing his father loved him, and who had the feeling of being integrated into his father's life. His dad would get a call in the middle of the night—that an alarm had gone off at the school, or that they couldn't find a bus driver for the football team—so he would have to get up and respond to the need. He would take Ernest along with him, at three, four, five, six years old.

At the same time, Ernest's father was also driven, demanding, and at times stubborn. When his dad determined that something needed to be done, he was absorbed in it, Ernest tells me, and you really couldn't push back. Some of the biggest challenges or frustrations or blowups were when someone challenged him or pushed back against his plan, no matter how big or small.

"I can laugh about it now, but it created this dynamic where, even when I knew I should say something or push back, I was reluctant to do so," Ernest reflects. "I wasn't afraid of him. I loved him and the joy of our relationship so much that I didn't want to do anything that would disrupt that equilibrium. So instead of pushing back on something that I knew would agitate him, I would hold it in and keep quiet."

And of the many times Ernest did not speak up, there is one that he regrets—one that will stick with him the rest of his life.

Staying Silent

Ernest's father loved to cook, and he loved to eat. His mother cooked most of the time, but when his father cooked, it was exotic. He loved to try new dishes. On the night of June 30, 1998, he kept it basic and made a steak dinner.

When he came home from work that night, he first took Ernest to Sonic. He loved their foot-long hotdogs, and they shared one as a snack. "Then we came home, and he made steak and potatoes for my mom and me. After we ate, my dad said, 'Come on. Let's get in the truck.' He had an old Chevy that he loved and he had just had some work done to it. He wanted to test it on the road because we would be going out of town."

When they got on the highway, the truck began to sputter. Engine troubles. Ernest's father took the next exit and turned around and headed back home. They were not far from the house, but Ernest was still concerned that the truck wouldn't make it on the highway, and he wanted to tell his father to pull over at the service station instead of getting back on the highway. The service station wasn't open, but its parking lot would at least be a safe place to pull off the road. Then they could turn off the truck and figure out what to do.

Ernest thought about telling his dad to pull over into the parking lot of the gas station. But he was reluctant to agitate his father. Ernest believed he would get upset or at least be dismissive of his son's suggestion.

So he kept his mouth shut.

It's clearly hard for him to talk about what comes next. Recounting traumatic events of childhood can place us right back in the moment—a moment that replays in our own heads but that is still painful to talk about. Often we simply choose not to share so as to avoid feeling it all over again.

Ernest leans forward, clasps his hands, and begins telling the story. "When we got back on the highway, we made it about halfway to the next exit, and the truck completely stalled in a construction zone on the interstate," Ernest tells me. "There were concrete barriers that boxed us in. Only a lane and a half was available for cars to pass, and several did. But we were in a dangerous position, and I was nervous while thinking *I'm not going to say anything.*"

After a short time, Ernest instinctively unbuckled his seatbelt and cracked open the door. His initial thought was that they should get out of the truck and stand on the median. "That is what I wanted to say, but again, I didn't," he says. "Twice in a two-minute period, I wanted to say something, but I didn't. I couldn't. I looked through the back window and saw a van approaching. It was coming fast. I had an instinct that it was not going to stop or go around us. It was going to hit us."

The van came up so fast that Ernest didn't have time to say or do anything. He had opened his door slightly as he wrestled with suggesting to his dad that they get out and stand on the median. But it was too late. In an instant, the van collided with the truck. Because his door was slightly open, the force of the impact thrust Ernest out of the truck and onto the ground. He heard the sound of metal crashing behind him.

Both vehicles were severely damaged, and his dad's truck hit the concrete barrier. Ernest ran up to the truck and looked through the window, where he saw the most horrifying image of his life. "I saw my dad take his last breath," Ernest tells me simply. So much devastation and sadness is contained in that sentence.

Ernest and I sit silently for a moment, as the weight of what he saw that day presses down. "It is a devastating vision that is branded in my memory, like a tattoo," he says finally, breaking the silence. "I was thirteen. Even in my youth, I knew the severe trauma would affect my life forever. I would never be the same."

Trauma Changes You

The loss of his dad changed Ernest in many ways. The thirteen years they had together were well spent. The bond they shared and the overwhelming influence he had on Ernest can be seen in the man he has become. Committed to helping others and treating everyone with respect and dignity, successful in his career, Ernest is a man of his word. Over the course of time that I have known Ernest, we have shared meals, attended conferences, and gone deep-sea fishing in Florida. I have admired the way Ernest engages people after speaking at a conference, making eye contact, sharing a smile, and shaking each person's hand. During business meetings, I watch him as he talks to leaders and takes an interest in the person. During dinners, he greets the waiter and remembers the person's name and treats them as if they were a friend.

In all these ways, Ernest is very much like his dad. "I definitely inherited his joy for intellectual banter," he says. "I have been very similar to him in fostering vast and diverse interpersonal relationships. He was a master at that, and I've tried to become more conscious of it."

As an educator, his father instilled in Ernest a love for learning. His father envisioned that, one day, the two of them would go into business together. One day over a meal, Ernest's father said, "When you go to college, I'll go to law school, and I will be finishing about the same time as you. I'll get the practice started and then send you to law school, and when you graduate, we'll have this practice together." They never got that far with that plan, but Ernest remained committed to becoming a leader and is very successful in his own right.

Ernest still longs for the presence of his dad. Even moments of celebration after an accomplishment are accompanied by a tinge of lament. "When I think about love, I wish my dad were still here," he says. Grief became the fuel for relentless ambition and Ernest's commitment to professional success. I get the sense that being so driven was also a way for Ernest to escape being still long enough to feel. "I never really grieved for him," he admits.

Whether we acknowledge it or not, experiences in our childhoods influence our behavior and how we show up in the world. Not only did Ernest become determined to succeed; he became determined to speak up. The "what if" thinking—*What if I had spoken up and suggested that he pull over?*—caused Ernest to express his viewpoint from that day forward, no matter the outcome, good or bad. Silence was not an option. "I promised myself that I would not be quiet any longer," Ernest reflects, "that I would speak up if I felt there was something that needed to be addressed, that needed to be said, regardless of the consequence."

The scenarios that play out in our heads about experiences we wish had turned out differently do not serve us well. They can cause us to punish ourselves by creating alternative outcomes that only exist in our imaginations. But those scenarios of regret are not based on reality and exclude the dynamics we were faced with in the moment. We can end up living in a past-driven present. This can result in filtering the present—which is all we really have—through the lens of past pain.

Gratitude and Healing from Grief

As Ernest shares the story of his dad with me, he pivots to talking about how his father handled feedback. He sits up in the chair with perfect posture and speaks with confidence. "I can say with a smile that my father likely would not have listened to me anyway. He would have forged ahead as he saw fit. That was who he was." Ernest is now able to interpret the traumatic experience through the lens of who he is now, as an adult, rather than through the eyes of the thirteen-year-old child.

I've found this to be important when working to heal an emotional childhood wound. When we reflect on the pain of the past, we often approach those memories as if we are still a vulnerable child. We end up feeling what we felt back then, as if that's still the person we are right now. The healthier approach is to position yourself as if you are on the outside of the story, reflecting on the memory and on the child you once were. You are not the same person that you were back then.

What happened in the past is a part of you, but it doesn't have the right to control the rest of your life. Healing happens when we confront the reality of what was, and when we grieve it, forgive ourselves, and express gratitude for the life we have today. We can choose to embrace this opportunity by valuing every moment of every day. For we know just how fragile the journey can be.

The thirteen years Ernest and his father had together were amazing, he says. Ernest's father was energetic, compassionate, and fully present with his son and everyone he met. He enjoyed life and did his best to get the most out of every moment of every day.

Ernest and I sit silently for a moment. It's as if an overwhelming sense of gratitude fills the room. "My dad's love absorbed me, and my admiration for him will always be with me," he says. "I am building better relationships and doing the emotional work that allows me to more fully integrate all parts of myself—giving myself permission to feel, express gratitude, and enjoy the journey of life."

The Past Lives On in Marriages

I am curious if Ernest sees any ways in which childhood experiences show up in his marriage. Watching Ernest and his wife, Keneta, smile and laugh together, you can tell they are best friends. Can Ernest remember moments with his wife in which he may have unknowingly acted like his dad? I ask.

There is a lot in the relationship with his wife to be unpacked, Ernest tells me. The relational dynamic that brought them together is that his wife appreciated his strong decision-making skills because that is not her orientation. "Even our wedding: I planned most aspects of our wedding and even where we have lived or moved," he says. "She really defaulted to my ability to make clear decisions, and she has told me that part of what she likes about me is my ability to make decisions and figure things out."

But even in her appreciation of his definitive approach, she does have her limits. Keneta doesn't want him to make all the decisions; when it comes to personal decisions that are just about the two of them, or when negotiating the dynamics of everyday life, she wants a say. Ernest had to learn to be different from his dad, and to recognize the times he was operating in a way that silenced his wife's voice.

While listening to Ernest, I think about how he didn't speak up as a child because experience taught him that his voice wasn't going to matter. I listen to him share about his resistance to negotiation early on in his marriage, and I wonder if, in some ways, his wife was experiencing the same feelings that he had felt as a child. Had she felt that her voice didn't matter to him, just as he had felt his voice hadn't mattered to his father?

We don't always communicate with our spouses in the ways that they need but instead act out what our childhood narratives have taught us to do. Like Ernest, I learned about communication through the trauma of my childhood experiences. I learned to be distant and share little, if anything, about my feelings. Listening to Ernest now, I realize that whenever I communicate with my son through the broken parts of my story, I am turning *him* into *my* wounded child. In those moments, he is experiencing the same sadness and isolation that I felt.

I share my personal revelation with Ernest, and he says that may very well have been the case for Keneta during the early years of their marriage. "When I think about the dynamics of my childhood, the death of my dad, I realize that I suppressed so much of the emotional side of who I am."

The impact of losing his dad had led Ernest to believe that emotion and sensitivity had absolutely no place in anything that he set out to do. He says that he consistently chose logic over expressions of love—and that it almost ended his marriage.

Pivoting from Pain

Like many people whose drive to succeed is propelled by past pain, Ernest eventually hit a wall. Ernest tells me he found himself wrestling with stress, anxiety, and latent depression. While he eventually accepted that the only way to find peace was through addressing the sadness within, even then he wanted to do it alone. Ernest attempted to push his wife away—and that's when things changed, he tells me.

"I remember sitting with my wife at this time when I was at rock bottom, and I wanted to cut and run. I wanted to leave our relationship, and everything about my life up to that point. It wasn't driven by any issue in our relationship. But everything about who I had become—well, I didn't want to be those things anymore. So I thought I had to totally separate myself."

Success had been Ernest's attempt to heal the pain of losing his dad. It wasn't working, and he wanted to walk away from everything. Achievement had failed to deliver on the hope of healing.

Knowing her husband better than anyone else, Keneta took that opportunity to use her voice. This time, he says, he knew that silencing her was not an option. As he tried to explain the logic for leaving, she interrupted him. "I know you are hurting, I know you are in pain, and I know there is something going on that I don't fully understand," she told him. "But I'm not going to let you do that. I'm not going to let you walk away. Whatever you need to do to figure it out, to come to yourself, I support you. I will give you that space. But you don't have permission to leave."

Those words—*You don't have permission to leave*—felt like someone had just thrown a glass of cold water in his face. It wasn't simply the shock of someone telling him that he didn't have permission to do something he thought he wanted to do; her words conveyed a deep and unconditional love.

At that moment, Ernest realized that he already had the thing that he was searching for through success: love. By telling him that he didn't have permission to leave, Keneta was showing Ernest that another person in his life was already filling the void of love left by the loss of his dad. She loved him deeply, and she was not going anywhere.

"Her words stopped me in my tracks," Ernest tells me. "By standing up to me in this deeply emotional and vulnerable way, she reignited a fire in me—an emotional fire, a deep love for her that was deeper than anything I knew I could experience. Her refusal to let me go deepened my love for her beyond what I thought possible. And it also caused me to recognize that I had been suppressing the emotional side of myself—to the point that if I didn't address it, it would literally destroy my life."

From that day on, Ernest says, he made the conscious decision to begin to rebuild the emotional side of himself that he had suppressed. Ernest is still on a journey of becoming more self-aware, learning to see the connection between the past and present, and making changes along the way. "Until our conversation, I don't think I ever connected the dots between who I am, who my dad was, and the work that I am continuing to do," Ernest tells me. "The process of reflecting on the sentence 'I wish my dad …' helped me connect the dots around who I was at thirteen years old, when my dad died, and how I began to suppress the compassionate part of myself."

The conversation also helped Ernest identify how a relentless quest for success can diminish the emotional aspects of life. "That, ironically, limited my ability to live in the success and enjoy it," he tells me. "I can also see the impact on my sense of happiness and fulfillment, and my relationship with my wife and others. I don't think I ever connected it all in the way that this conversation gave me the opportunity to do."

Takeaways

Ernest's "I Wish My Dad" story demonstrates the benefit of empowering a son's voice. Ernest's father instilled in him a self-confidence that powerfully assisted him in his development as a man. When fathers value the way their sons think and feel, it conveys confidence in their cognitive processing. This allows sons to develop a capacity for strong leadership.

When a father stunts his son's ability to freely voice his concerns or opinions, it does the opposite. A son learns to suppress his feelings and often finds himself in a lifelong quest to gain his father's trust and approval.

The tragic loss of his father caused Ernest to carry the anguish of *What if I had spoken up?* And because of that, he grew to be hypervigilant about expressing himself, which did not always serve him well.

You can end up projecting your traumatic childhood experience onto the people you love. Sometimes it's important to pause and ask, *Am I doing to others what was done to me?* Remember how it felt when your own voice was silenced. How did it feel when you believed what you had to say didn't matter? That's the same feeling others experience at your hands if you've begun to believe that speaking up takes precedence over judgment and concern for others' feelings. Another question to ask yourself is: *How can I respond to others in a way that offers others what I once needed?*

When fathers empower sons, it communicates that they are valued and that their thoughts and opinions matter. When fathers break a cycle, they free themselves from the past and allow their sons—and themselves—to thrive in the present.

CHAPTER 2

I WISH MY DAD ALLOWED ME TO SHARE MY FEELINGS

PHIL

When I mentioned that I was writing a book about the power of vulnerable conversations between fathers and sons, my friend Philipia held up a hand to stop me partway through my description. "Wait," she interrupted. "You definitely need to interview my dad. He has a story I think you should hear."

So I did. Phil, who is in his early seventies, grew up in Chicago. He is a no-nonsense kind of guy. He's all about getting things done and doing them with excellence. Phil also has a soft heart for people; he's a caring person who will push you to do better while at the same time offering to help. Phil is a person of faith who is committed to the church he attends and serves on several community boards.

As a labor leader and president of the only Black postal service employees union in Chicago, Phil's dad had a commitment to social change that wasn't simply work—it was a way of life. His values guided his actions, and work and home life often intersected. "Our house was always full of traffic," Phil remembers.

"One of my memories is of people coming by and needing to talk about things like negotiating labor issues. I remember sitting and listening in the background to how my father would manage and talk to people." His father was a person everyone looked up to, and Phil looked up to him too. People trusted his leadership and followed his guidance.

But like so many fathers, Phil's dad was unable to give his son everything he longed to receive, including the assurance that he'd be loved and valued even if he didn't meet his father's supremely high expectations.

As Phil and I talk about his father and their relationship, I am struck by the ways that adult sons often still seek to justify their fathers' unhealthy behavior. We often want to give our dads the benefit of the doubt. There's nothing wrong with that, but sometimes our unwillingness to see our father's failures isn't helpful. When our fathers are our heroes, we as grown men have trouble naming the ways our fathers failed us. It's like we become little boys again when we think and talk about our dads—unwilling or unable to take a hard look at what we longed for but didn't receive.

Family Pride

Throughout most of his life, Phil has wanted to follow in his footsteps because he respected and admired his dad. His own family values and involvement in the community and church stem from what was modeled by his dad.

Phil's dad's life was guided by going to church, being a family man, and caring for his community. When it came to family, he had clear expectations. "He always wanted to instill family values in me," Phil says. "Everything revolved around what was best for the family and family pride. He had this thing: you're a Hillman, and that means something." His dad's approach instilled confidence in Phil, and he has always taken pride in being a member of his family.

Phil's dad had high expectations for his children as well. Doing well in school was a must. His sister, who is fourteen years older than Phil, got the first PhD in the family. "Dad instilled that. He told her after she graduated from college, 'I love the fact you got your degree, but you need to do more.'" Phil remembers when he got his undergraduate degree in chemistry. "I was pretty proud of that because a lot of people don't get such technical degrees," Phil says. "But my dad said, 'That's good, son. Now when are you getting your master's?'"

Phil smiles. He did eventually get his master's degree. There was a lot of pressure to do well, but Phil wanted to make his father proud. Slacking off was not an option.

During his sophomore year in high school, Phil quickly learned that his dad meant what he said. Phil was a talented athlete, and he was on the wrestling team. His grades dropped that year from As and Bs to Bs and Cs. "Dad knew my grades dropped, and one day he came up to the school while I was in wrestling practice," Phil recounts. "He walked over to the coach and said, 'I'm pulling my son off the team because his grades have dropped. When his grades get back up, then I will talk about whether he can come back on the team.'"

Phil was shocked. He couldn't believe his dad was willing to go that far. The coach tried to work things out with Phil's dad, but it was not up for discussion.

Phil's dad saw himself as the provider for the household. Like many men of his generation, he displayed love through provision, not affection. "My dad wasn't a hugger. I call it the John Wayne Syndrome: You take care of business, and you don't need help as a man of the house," Phil reflects. "Love looked like, *You know I love you. Now go perform, do more, get it done.* He set very high standards, and when you didn't meet the standards, there wasn't a whole lot of sympathy."

When his father was not happy with Phil, he had a way of making him feel guilty. "It was always, *You're not working hard enough. Son, you're letting the family down here. What about the family, son?* That was his way of trying to motivate me." Listening to Phil, I can't help but wonder whether the pressure of meeting his dad's expectations brought about unhealthy shame and guilt. But Phil had a high level of respect for his dad and wanted to please him. "I knew that family meant everything to him. I was so invested in him being right that I would simply turn and say, 'I've got to step up. I have to do better.'"

Thus Phil remained committed to his dad's idea of performing for the family at all costs. Thinking his dad was right, Phil put a higher priority on meeting his father's expectations than on letting himself consider what would happen if he failed.

As we sit together in my office now, I tell Phil that I think his dad put too much pressure on him. What were the costs of being compelled to comply and get it right for his dad?

The room falls silent. Phil sits there staring at me for a moment, looking both shocked and sad.

"The reason I am staring at you is that it just occurred to me that I did some of that with my son," he says. "I think sometimes I put that whole thing about expectations of the family on him. That is exactly what I did to him."

Needing Dad to Love without Judgment

Phil's dad didn't say the words "I love you" very often. The way Phil knew that he was loved was that his dad was consistently present. In any difficult situation, he always showed up. A particular memory surfaces when he thinks about his dad being there for him. Phil had been accused of stealing a bike. "I'll never forget that day," he tells me. "Someone saw me standing near a bike, and later some guy stole that same bike. The police took me down to the police station, and my dad came with me."

At the police station, the officers interviewed Phil, who was a minor at the time, without his father in the room. The police told him they were going to take him from his parents and put him in a home for juvenile delinquents. They were trying to intimidate him into confessing. Phil was terrified. "Tears were coming down my cheeks, when all of the sudden the door of the office flew open and my dad walked in. He looked at me and said, 'Son, did you steal that bike?' I said, 'No, sir.'"

Phil's father took him by the hand, looked at the officer, and said, "Unless you have some evidence, I'm taking my son out of here." Phil smiles at the memory. "We walked out of that station. I thought my dad was ten feet tall that day."

As Phil tells the story, I can sense how proud he is of his dad. His father stood up for him because he believed his son. He may not have said "I love you," but he expressed it through his actions. When Phil talks about what love from his dad looked like, he focuses on what his father provided. And the story of his father's belief in him, and the way he stood up to the police officers, is a moving example of a father's love.

But I want to know if there was anything else that Phil needed. What did he need to feel loved well by his dad?

Instead of talking about his own longings, Phil continues to share how he benefited from his dad's approach. It's like he can't yet see his own needs; his father looms too large in the space between my question and any possible answer. So I press him on the question again. I want to know how he needed to be treated to feel loved more deeply by his dad. I want him to think about *his* needs, not just his father's rationale.

Phil pauses, as if going through memories in his mind. "For me, love could have looked like: *I am there for you when you are struggling, and I won't judge you when you are struggling. I will just be there for you.*" He thinks for another moment. "I wish my dad would have loved me more without judging as much."

Rather than being told that he let the family down when he made mistakes, Phil says his dad could have expressed his disappointment but also encouraged him in the same conversation. "It was always about what I could have done better. But there were times when I needed to hear *It's okay, son*. I needed to be comforted sometimes. I know his concept was that men were strong, tough, and didn't need that type of comfort," he says. "But we actually do."

The Absolute Ruler

Strength: it's a common idea of manhood. Phil describes his dad's definition of strength as taking care of business, not asking for help, getting things done, working hard, and making no excuses for mistakes. Feelings, or any aspect of the interior life, are not a part of the definition of strength for many men. Joy and happiness are often seen as naïve because of a belief that life is hard and you need to be tough. And how about expressing sadness, disappointment, or fear? Those are seen as signs of weakness and not being tough enough. This idea of manhood comes with a lot of pressure, unspoken worry about failing, and the weight of holding in feelings to maintain the image of being strong.

As Phil and I talk about his "I Wish My Dad" story, I tell him that being strong and being vulnerable don't stand in opposition to each other. Being strong and expressing feelings of sadness or fear or loneliness do not mean that a man isn't strong. It just means that he allows himself to be fully human. Vulnerability does not have to be sacrificed on the altar of manhood and achievement.

Phil listens carefully and nods his head. "I would agree with that. And when I think about what I needed from my dad, I think I just simply needed to hear *I love you*. He wasn't big on saying it. It was almost like: *You know I love you. I take care of you. I'm in your corner*." The weight of unspoken love has come up in several of my conversations with men about their fathers, and here it is again. "I could point to all the things that he did," Phil says. "But I would have preferred the words sometimes. I would have liked for him to hug me and say *I love you; we'll get through this*."

When Phil got older, he began initiating hugs with his father. "He was fine with it," Phil remembers. "He didn't resist it. I think it actually put a smile on his face."

Judgment did not provide Phil with a road map for how to handle mistakes and overcome challenges. Advice on how to pick himself back up after a failure, or stories of times that his father had gotten knocked down in life and how he had gotten back up—those would have given him far more useful tools than the weight of shaming and judgment.

Phil and one of his friends—someone he's known since second grade who was the best man at Phil's wedding and later godfather to his sons—had a name for this type of father. "We grew up at each other's house all the time," Phil says. "We both labeled our fathers, who we thought of as identical. We used to call them A.R.: Absolute Rulers. That is how we saw them: absolute rulers who rule absolutely." The absolute ruler's word was law. Their dads didn't talk about love or affection. It was do as I say, watch what I do—and fall in line.

Phil's dad made all the decisions about Phil's life, what he could and couldn't do. His mind was made up on who Phil was going to become, and Phil didn't have a say in it. He shares a story with me of what that looked like.

When Phil was in college, he participated in boxing and wrestling and was great at both. Phil was in a boxing tournament and was a lot better than people in his weight class.

When the finals came and the coach was pairing people off, there was a guy Phil had never seen before. The coach paired up Phil with the new guy in the class, and they fought for three rounds. "Afterwards the coach came up to me and said, 'I didn't tell you this, but that guy trains for the Olympics. And you are actually better than he is. If you don't mind, I would like to come by and talk to your dad about getting you into the program, because I think you have that kind of ability.'"

The coach stopped by Phil's house to have a conversation with his dad about getting him into the boxing program. Phil was excited. He was twenty years old and already married, but he and his wife were living in his parents' house. His dad—the A.R.—still had the final word. The coach told his dad what happened during the fight and how well Phil had performed against a guy training for the Olympics. His dad listened as the coach spoke, and then finally broke his silence. He said his son was not going to be a fighter. "I'm sending my son to school to get an education," his father said. His mind was already made up about who Phil was going to be.

Phil sat there listening to the conversation between the coach and his father. "I sat there, and tears came to my eyes as I listened to Dad say, 'No, no sorry. He is not a fighter. He is going to be a doctor.' He got the coach up and walked him to the door and let him out."

The absolute ruler who ruled absolutely had spoken.

Family Dinner or Board Meeting?

Phil's dad lived an extraordinary life, but Phil never learned a lot about his story. Many of the things he knows about his dad were things told to him by people who knew him. For example, his father's buddies sometimes said that he could have played in the major leagues. Phil's dad would take Phil to Chicago Cubs games to watch their favorite player, Ernie Banks. "Ernie Banks actually came by the house, but I didn't get to talk to him," Phil recalls. "But I listened as he and my dad talked."

Phil's dad had a lot of influence in Chicago. "We had Martin Luther King come by my house one time, and we have a picture hanging in the basement of my mom and Martin Luther King," Phil says. He has always wanted to know the backstory of the meeting that took place in their home. Quality time would have looked like his dad sharing stories like that, from his work in the community, challenges in the labor movement, and his relationships with other leaders.

When Phil did get time with his dad, it was often at the dinner table. That's where most of their conversations took place. But the dinner hour was like a board meeting, Phil recalls. "The dinner table was sacrosanct. You needed to have a real reason to be away for dinner, because that's where the Absolute Ruler reaffirmed expectations. It was important to be present, because after dinner he was off to another meeting." Phil is silent for a moment, as if he is prompting himself to go deeper. "I wish my dad had included conversations about his day, stories about meetings, and shared his feelings. That would have made me happy because I would have known him as a person much better."

A Hug from Dad Would Have Changed Everything

Of all the stories Phil shared with me, one hurt the most to hear. Once Phil was playing in a church basketball league, and his team was competing in the championship game. Phil was the point guard, and his team was up by one point. The other team had the ball. "I had issues with one of the guys on the other team. Every time he would run through a pick, because I had a knee brace on, he would bend his knee a little bit to hit my knee," he says.

Phil's team was up by one, but the other team had the ball and a chance to take the lead. They got the shot they wanted and missed. The ball was passed to Phil. Up by one, with ten seconds left on the clock, Phil knew that all he had to do was let time run out and his team would win the championship. The guy who had been trying to hit Phil's knee came over to guard him.

"I looked up: nine seconds. I was not going to move. I knew they had to come foul me. Well, the guy didn't foul me; he dove and tackled me," Phil says. "He hit my knee and tackled me. I got up and punched him, and the refs threw us both out of the game."

Phil's team got two free throw attempts and the other team got one. With Phil on the bench after being ejected from the game for throwing a punch, his replacement had to shoot the free throws. He missed both free throws, and the guy on the other team made his. The game was tied and went into overtime, with Phil sitting on the bench. The other team won.

After the game, Phil walked outside and looked around the parking lot for the car. But his dad had driven off and had left him there. "I had to take the bus home," Phil recalls. "It wasn't a big deal taking the bus home, but he had brought me to the game, and he hadn't told me he was leaving. He just left me. And I knew why he left me. Because at the end of the day, that loss was my fault."

Leaving was apparently his dad's way of imposing judgment and shame for failing. "I was so distraught sitting on that bench, and I wanted a hug," Phil says. "I wanted a hug because I was in tears. I felt like I had let the team down."

Phil tells me that he often shares that story with his sons as a lesson about controlling their tempers and maintaining composure in tough situations. That's what Phil wishes he had done in the game. I'm sitting there, stunned, as I listen to Phil describe the takeaway from the story that he extracts for his sons. What about his dad leaving him behind? What about the choices that fathers make to judge and shame rather than support and nurture?

Phil is still missing it, I think—and I tell him so. Yes, he made a mistake, but he still needed his dad at that moment, I tell him. What he needed from his dad—and failed to receive—is the real heart of this story. That's the real source of sadness.

Phil and I sit together in silence as that sinks in. He begins to see my point. "Looking back now, I wish he would have been there for me after the game," he admits. "I wish he could have just said, 'Son, maybe you learned something tonight. But it's going to be okay.'"

The lesson in this story, for Phil and for all of us, lies in understanding what sons need when they make mistakes. The lesson can't be about justifying fathers' judgment or inability to give their sons what they need. I say that as a father, and I know how easy it is to make split-second parenting decisions that you later regret.

But Phil's eagerness to excuse his father for failing in that moment doesn't change the fact of what he as a son needed. What Phil needed was to lay his head on his dad's shoulder, cry, and receive a hug.

Although Phil's own three children are adults now, fathers never lose the opportunity to make changes. Phil recognizes the times that he let his father's style of parenting become his own. "But I'm learning that my kids are who they are, and I have to acknowledge that they have a right to make their own choices," he says. "That's something I wish my dad had done for me. I would have loved for him to say once in a while, 'Well, how do you feel and what do *you* want to do?'"

Takeaways

Phil's "I Wish My Dad" story is filled with the challenges of living with an absolute ruler in the home. This type of fathering came with the expectation of perfectionism. Perfectionism often stems from a sense of inadequacy or failure. I wonder what blame, judgment, or shame Phil's father was protecting himself from as he imbued the same feelings in Phil.

Phil's dad fathered from a place of fear—hence the pressure he placed on Phil to perform and uphold the family name. If he as a father didn't rule absolutely, he was afraid that Phil would fail. Phil was not given an opportunity to individuate in his adolescence and early adulthood, to become his own person. What greatness and uniqueness do fathers kill in their sons when they project expectations of themselves onto them? What if Phil had decided to go to the Olympic training boxing program as his coach suggested? Who would Phil be if he was encouraged to make mistakes and learn from them?

When sons are given an opportunity to discover, they are able to deepen their own understanding of themselves and become more aware of their capacities. Phil's healing journey has brought him to the awareness that his children have a right to make their own choices. Phil is learning to validate his own children's feelings and to offer them a flexibility and understanding that he did not receive.

CHAPTER 3

I WISH MY DAD AFFIRMED MY VALUE

MICHAEL-RAY

Michael-Ray and I first met when I was a consultant doing strategy for clients and he was an organizer for a national faith-based organization. Over time we shared stories about wounds from our childhoods. We were both working to heal through therapy, and we opened up to each other about what we were learning. I knew that he was someone I could trust with my story, and I'm grateful he was willing to trust me with his.

Michael-Ray cares deeply about making life better for vulnerable and poor communities. There's no such thing as a shallow conversation with Michael-Ray. As deputy director for a global faith-based community organizing network, podcast host, and former pastor, Michael-Ray is not interested in what people do. He's interested in who people are and what they value and what they stand for. Michael-Ray is fifty-two years old, from Compton, California. He and his wife, Dene Murray-Mathews, have one child, Kenan, who is a young adult. After hearing his story, I realize how easily his life could have taken a different turn and hardened him. But somehow, by the grace of God, his childhood journey gave him the gift of empathy.

Michael-Ray's relationship with his dad, who was not affectionate or warm toward his son, was fraught with challenges. At his father's funeral, Michael-Ray listened as family members and others who knew him talked about how his dad had been like a father to them. Michael-Ray was stunned. The man everyone else knew as a good, caring father figure stood in stark contrast to who he was for his son.

How could a man remembered by acquaintances and friends as a compassionate listener and thoughtful mentor be so cold and hardened at home? How do our fathers sometimes offer gifts of presence and care to others that they couldn't extend to us?

When a Son Is a Mirror

Michael-Ray's dad was just starting to figure out how to be a father when he passed away, at age forty-nine. He had been an alcoholic for a long time, but the last nine years of his life were years of sobriety. As he talks about his father's battles with alcoholism, Michael-Ray reflects on the issues his father grappled with over the years that were likely underlying his drinking.

"I think my dad had a lot of deep issues," Michael-Ray says, "from growing up in an alcoholic family, to growing up in poverty in rural Louisiana, to growing up as a Black man in the 1950s and 1960s, to going to Vietnam." Michael-Ray is a thoughtful person just like his dad was, and he sees clearly what shaped his father. "He had a lot of insecurities about a lot of things—things he relied on the bottle to help him deal with."

Michael-Ray's dad was verbally abusive, sometimes using derogatory terms about female body parts to talk about his son. He seemed very disappointed in Michael-Ray, and it was years before he realized that beneath his dad's verbal abuse was fear.

"It was very, very painful and took me a long time to really come to terms with that," Michael-Ray muses. "He was very critical of me. He was very worried about how soft I am. He was really worried about me being called gay or a sissy."

Michael-Ray's dad was fearful for his safety. "I think he also feared for himself, because I think all of those qualities that he was critiquing in me were his. The more I talked to people in the family, the more I learned how they saw him as sensitive and effeminate."

The verbal abuse that Michael-Ray endured left him with self-doubt and insecurities. He is very much aware of what he needed from his dad that would have helped him navigate life with confidence: affirmation, encouragement, and compassionate touch. Being hugged by his dad in difficult times would have helped soothe the pain.

Michael-Ray shares a story of a time he needed his dad to hug him and affirm his value. "One day after school I was headed home, and some guy was calling me a fag and beat me up," Michael-Ray recounts. "My dad asked what happened, so I told him. His response? 'You should have won the fight. Maybe you *are* a fag if you couldn't fight him.'"

So at eleven years old, Michael-Ray learned that he couldn't trust that he was safe in his neighborhood or at home. The rejection from his father caused him to withdraw even more, both physically and emotionally.

Looking back at that day now, Michael-Ray concludes that his father saw the incident—his son getting beat up—as a critique of *him*, as the parent. If his son couldn't defend himself, that must mean he was not parenting him properly. But the reality is the opposite. Instead of prompting him to look at himself, that incident was an opportunity to think about what his son needed from him. What did that eleven-year-old boy need at that moment? How could he, as his father, provide it?

As an adult, Michael-Ray now has the words to describe what he needed that day that he didn't receive from his father. "I needed him to say, 'I'm sorry you got beat up. It hurts. It's okay for you to cry because it hurts. It's okay for you to talk about how afraid you were, how helpless you felt, how angry you are, how you wish you had hit that motherf*cker back.'"

Emotionally, Michael-Ray needed his dad to offer healing language. "I needed him to tell me that what happened to me was not right. I needed him to say, 'It's going to be okay, and you are going to be okay.'"

After being physically assaulted, Michael-Ray needed his dad to reaffirm the value of his body. He was physically wounded, and words of affirmation and the compassionate touch of a hug would have sent the message to him that his body has value and is worthy of love, not violence. A hug would have been a part of the healing process to address the emotional pain he was feeling.

But sons are sometimes like mirrors for fathers—a reflection of the pain fathers never dealt with from their own childhood. Michael-Ray's father didn't know what to do with that pain, and as a result, he imposed that pain on his son. Perhaps he was afraid that Michael-Ray would have to endure the same rejection and isolation that he had faced when he was growing up, but in his attempt to harden his son and make him tougher, he ended up inflicting pain and feelings of isolation.

Trying to Figure It Out

Michael-Ray says that his dad never hugged him while he was growing up. He wanted to hear the words "I love you" from his father. "I have no memory of him hugging me. No memory of him saying he loved me. None."

Michael-Ray and his dad avoided each other, from puberty all the way up to when he was nineteen years old. When the time came for college, he moved out of the family home. He went to USC in Los Angeles, only a twenty-five-minute drive from Compton, where he grew up. When Michael-Ray moved out, his mom talked his dad into giving him the family car. The car ended up becoming a way for him and his dad to be in a relationship with each other. His dad had been teaching himself to work on cars, and he would drive out to where Michael-Ray lived in LA, where they would work on the car together and then go out for breakfast. Those moments were his father's expressions of love, Michael-Ray recognizes now, and he is passing on this particular expression of love to his own son. "To this day, communion for me and my son is going to breakfast," Michael-Ray says. "We call it 'hanging with the Pops.' We started calling it that when I was in a restaurant with my young son and someone turned and said to my little boy, 'So, you hanging with the Pops?' So that's our thing now."

While Michael-Ray was in college, his dad would call from time to time and ask if he wanted to go to the movies. He'd pick up his son and they would head out to the movie theater. Working on the car together, going to breakfast, and watching movies: these were his dad's way of trying to figure out how to be in his son's life, particularly after he had moved out. Michael-Ray appreciated the effort his dad was making.

But Michael-Ray desired deeper conversations too. He longed to be affirmed by his dad. "I needed him to tell me that I was okay as I was—sensitive and effeminate," he says. "I wanted him to tell me that I was going to be all right, that I could face challenges in front of me. I think he wanted to and maybe even tried to say those things. But it was hard for him to be direct in the way that I needed it."

Michael-Ray believes his dad was trying to protect him from harm. He thought that he was helping his son become tough. He thought his son needed to "man up." But calling his son a "sissy" and other derogatory terms failed and resulted in a lot of trauma his son would have to heal later in life.

Michael-Ray and his dad were beginning to cultivate a new kind of relationship after he moved out, and that relationship accelerated when his dad was diagnosed with cancer.

Michael-Ray didn't receive the affection and affirmation he longed for, but a measure of healing did take place. He and his father spent time together creating healthy memories. He got to see that his dad was capable of embarking on a different kind of journey, and that he was making an effort. "I can say that my father and I were reconciled," he says. "The real blessing for me and for all of us in the tragedy of his passing at such a young age is that he had restored his relationship with my mom, that he had restored his relationship with me, and he was a much more present father to my sister and brother."

Michael-Ray's dad died ten months after he was diagnosed with cancer. Before he died, he called the family together. Gathered in the room were his wife, Michael-Ray, and his two younger siblings. To Michael-Ray he said, "I have treated you really poorly. And I don't know why."

That was such a bittersweet confession, reflects Michael. "On the one hand he was acknowledging that he treated me poorly. But it was also hard and infuriating to hear him say he didn't know why."

Sometimes sons have to figure out the answers to questions their fathers pose but can't answer themselves. How could his father love his children so much but treat them so poorly? How can fathers' love get so mangled along the way, between intention and action?

Two decades of therapy have helped Michael-Ray wrestle with his father's *why*.

Answering a Father's Why

Michael-Ray's journey in therapy started when he was in college and his dad was fighting cancer. His dad was dying, so Michael-Ray took a year off. Before leaving school, however, he took a counseling psychology class that required students to see a therapist. During that time his father died, and so his dad ended up being the focus of his work with the therapist.

Michael's therapist wanted to know if he could forgive his father. The question made Michael-Ray pause. "It was more like I was open to trying to understand who he was," he reflects now. "I probably had forgiveness language, but it wasn't really forgiveness yet."

It wasn't until his thirties that Michael-Ray began to understand his father's story: what made him who he was. At that time, Michael-Ray was about to become a father himself. His nights were restless, and he experienced intense nightmares. In his dreams he and his dad would have physical altercations. Their relationship in real life had been abusive but had never turned physical. Yet the dreams of physical altercations were very traumatic for Michael-Ray. He would wake up screaming, and his wife would have to calm him down.

Michael-Ray realized that he needed to see a therapist. He came to the realization that he was afraid of becoming a father. He was sure he would "mess up" a son the way his father had done with him, so Michael-Ray prayed for a daughter.

He had a son, though, and that fact prompted him to continue taking his own healing seriously. "During that time, I began to realize just how much learning to forgive my father was also about me learning to forgive myself," he tells me. "If I could learn to forgive myself and have grace with myself as a father, I would not have to fall into what I felt was a trap for my dad: his fear of intimacy with me. I wanted to be close to my son—and I am."

Only when he understood his father's story could he extend real forgiveness to his father. "I came to recognize that my dad did the best he could with what he had."

We Will Graduate from This

Michael-Ray abruptly stops our conversation. The room is silent for a moment, and I can tell by the serious look on his face that what he is about to say is difficult. There's a weight to what is coming.

"I haven't shared something important with you," he says to me. "I'm a survivor of sexual abuse." Michael tells me he was in kindergarten when he was assaulted. He never told his dad that he was sexually abused, but Michael-Ray is almost sure that his father knew he had been abused.

In many situations, sexual abuse carries the weight of such shame and secrecy that it prevents the protection of young people. "When I think about the stories and the adults around in our community: well, people knew," he says. "They *chose* not to know. They might honestly tell you they didn't know that someone was being abused, and they would think they were being honest. But they'd cut stuff off to protect themselves."

Michael-Ray says it's important to share that he is a survivor of sexual abuse because it gives people who know him not only a deeper lens into the work he has been doing to heal his sense of self but a look into why he is committed to loving his son well. "I made a decision that I was going to be affectionate with my son," he tells me firmly. "I was going to tell him I love him; I was going to kiss him; I was going to hug and hold him, and I wasn't going to worry about whether or not that would make him effeminate or weak or soft. I decided that would make him whole."

Looking at who his dad was as a man and a father, Michael-Ray was aware of what he had needed: affection and affirmation. Those were the things he was going to offer his son. Working on himself and trying to understand his dad were labors of healing. It was not about critiquing his dad.

Michael reflects on why he worked so hard in therapy. "We— my son and the family I started—are going to graduate from this," he says of the commitments he made back then. "We're going to change this tide. My son is going to hear *I love you*. He is going to know how to say it back to me. He's not going to be uncomfortable with that. It is not going to be a problem for him."

Michael-Ray's son Kenan is a young adult now, and he and his dad are very close. Michael-Ray gives his son lots of affirmation, love, and affection, and he is always reflecting on ways to make their relationship even better. "Kenan needs to know that I'm proud of him," Michael-Ray says. "I am trying to defeat this curse on us. So I made a commitment that my son was going to feel my love. I was going to hug and kiss him every night. When he was young, right before bed, I would rub his back in a circle and say, 'The Lord bless you and keep you. The Lord make his face to shine upon you and be gracious unto you. The Lord lift up his countenance upon you and give you peace, in Jesus's name, amen. Good night, son, I love you.'"

Michael-Ray smiles at the memory. "So I hadn't done that in a while. But when he dropped me off at the airport on my way to this interview, I rubbed his back in a circle. He looked at me, and I said, 'I'm not going to pray the whole prayer.' But I know that there is a physical memory in his body. That circle on his back means something."

Reconciling Rage

Michael-Ray did a lot of work in therapy to heal and forgive his dad. By the time his dad died, he felt that they had reconciled. But there was still some unfinished business he failed to address: the rage and grief about what he had not received from his dad. "During those four years that I call 'the reconciling years' with my dad, I never said, 'Dad, you hurt me. You hurt me when you did this or that. I am angry with you. Something was lost. I live in the world with fear and with shame because I didn't get love and affirmation from you. I didn't get that sense that I was okay in the world just as I am.'"

Reconciliation with his dad only focused on the present, and it didn't address the pain of the past. During those years before his father died, they were focused on the here and now and just being together. They never found a way to have transparent and confessional conversations about what had gone on in their relationship.

Michael-Ray suppressed his anger when his father was diagnosed, and he suppressed the anger after his father died. "I felt it was wrong to be angry now that he was gone," he says. But therapy helped him recognize that he still carried rage and grief that needed to be acknowledged. "I wouldn't be able to forgive him unless I could say *you hurt me*. I needed to name it. To give voice to the fact that he emotionally abandoned me."

One day his therapist asked him a strange question: "Have you apologized to your dad?" His father was dead, so the therapist didn't mean an actual conversation, but he was suggesting an imagined conversation. Michael-Ray didn't understand why an apology was necessary. In fact, the mere questions angered him.

"When the therapist asked if I had apologized to my dad, I said, 'For what?!' He said, 'For removing him from his rightful place in your life as your father. You removed him from that role, and you need to apologize to him.'"

Michael-Ray realized that, years earlier, he had indeed decided that his father's lack of love and affirmation wasn't going to define who he is. He had decided that he was going to shape his own identity and delete his dad entirely. He made an adjustment in their relationship: that he would no longer let his dad decide whether or not he was okay.

His therapist understood the adjustment he had made, but he explained to Michael-Ray that the decision to cut himself off from his dad was still playing out in his life—and it was not serving him well. Excluding his father, even in his mind, meant he was not able to be vulnerable and transparent in other relationships.

"I wasn't buying it—for a long time. I would drive to therapy sessions saying, 'I'm going to fire his ass today if he mentions my father one more time,'" Michael-Ray reflects now. "It took me a while to be open to the conversation, to recognize that there were ways in which removing my dad meant that I didn't have to be vulnerable anymore with anyone. That way I could be a protected person. I could walk in the world with a mask, and I could protect myself from judgment, from shame, from any questions about my manhood."

Cutting his dad off emotionally as a way to keep himself from being hurt, judged, or shamed had spread into other parts of his life. Forgiving his dad—and asking for forgiveness from his dad, even after he died—allowed Michael-Ray to release the anger he was holding. It helped him take down emotional walls he had built to keep his dad out—walls that were now keeping others out too.

Michael-Ray is now offering to Kenan what his father wouldn't—or couldn't—offer to him. He and his own son have graduated from the trauma that held back his relationship with his father. By exhibiting emotional flexibility with his son, Michael-Ray is breaking the cycle for himself and Kenan. Kenan will pass on the warmth, love, and care of his father to his own children someday, should he decide to have them. In this way, future generations are born into families that are a bit more whole than the previous ones.

Takeaways

Michael-Ray's "I Wish My Dad" story demonstrates how a father can project insecurities and unresolved trauma on a son who simply yearns to be seen, to be protected, and to experience affection and affirmation. Michael-Ray's father was emotionally neglectful and verbally abusive, which is a common and yet often overlooked form of abuse. Verbal abuse is aggressive behavior that occurs through spoken word. It can present as high criticism, threats, contemptuous language, and frequent belittling. Parents who are verbally abusive generally perceive it as "tough love." If childhood trauma remains unresolved, children exposed to verbal abuse can encounter bouts of depression, develop severe low self-esteem and confidence, and become more at risk for health issues, addictions, and future abusive behavior themselves.

Michael-Ray's father encountered what are called adverse childhood experiences (ACEs). These ACEs—such as racism, exposure to alcoholism, poverty, emotional neglect, and verbal abuse from his own father—coupled with his traumatic experiences in the Vietnam War—led Michael-Ray's father to split: to cut off parts of himself in order to survive. This is evidenced by the difference between his public persona as a loving and attentive man and his private persona as an emotionally abusive father who struggled with alcoholism.

Participating in his own healing work enabled Michael-Ray to be more present with his father from college through his father's last breath. It is a blessing that his father was able to own and acknowledge his mistreatment of Michael-Ray, and it is disappointing he could not do it sooner.

When we cut off parts of ourselves, we can become emotionally and spiritually abusive to ourselves and others. What type of father would Michael-Ray's father have been if he were able to love himself wholly? What type of father could you become if you chose to love yourself wholly?

CHAPTER 4

I WISH MY DAD LOVED MY MOM MORE

JOE

Joe is full of energy. He will always greet you with a smile, a hug, and a high-five—more like three high-fives within the first two minutes of a conversation. He's a big guy who sometimes forgets that your hand is a lot smaller than his, so his high-fives sting a little. But that's just Joe. Joe is an encourager with a big heart. He will make you feel better on a down day, do whatever he can to help, and make sure that you know you are valued and seen.

Joe is an author, a pastor, and founder of a community development organization. He is sixty-one years old and married to Madelyn. They have two children: Joia, thirty-three, and Joey, thirty-one. He has flown in from Washington, DC for our conversation, and when he arrives at my home, we hug, laugh, and exchange a few high-fives. We then head up to my office to talk.

When he sits down in the chair across from me, I get the sense that he is a little anxious. I offer him a bottle of water, setting it on the coffee table between us, and ask if he is ready to get started. "Yes, this is good, I've thought about it a lot on my way here," he says. "I'm ready."

Several years ago, Joe attended a seminar that I was hosting in Atlanta. One of the sessions dealt with pinpointing one sentence that describes how a person wants to be remembered. The exercise addresses how to clarify purpose in life. I helped Joe come up with the six-word sentence for how he wants to be remembered. His six words were: *I help broken people become whole.*

Now, after listening to him talk about his dad, I know why.

A Present Provider

Joe has a great deal of respect for his dad, who was a loving, caring, and hardworking provider. He had a heart for people on the margins of society. He was a passionate advocate for fairness, equity, and opportunity for all. He worked hard and made time to have fun, and Joe admired his dad for these qualities.

At the same time, his father was somewhat distant. He appeared to be an extrovert in social situations and was highly social with friends, but at home he was more of an introvert: often quiet, off to himself, and distant.

The two of them did spend lots of time together, doing things that many fathers enjoy doing with their sons, such as going to football games and other sporting events. Reflecting on the good times hanging out with his dad, Joe recalled when they lived in Philadelphia and went to see the Eagles. His dad took him to the Penn Relays, perhaps the biggest and most well-known track and field event in the country. Joe smiles as he recalls the day his father taught him to ride a bike, as well as how he worked with a friend to build Joe's first basketball goal in the yard using an old rusty pole and hoop. Joe would practice basketball almost every day and ended up playing in college years later. Here Joe pauses and begins to cry. "You probably have a lot of people crying in these moments. I'm starting to tear up. He was always there."

Yet despite these many fond memories of time spent with his dad, Joe desired to know his father much more. Psychologist Eric D. Miller writes that the emptiness within men, such as that Joe articulated to me, can be thought of as "a lack of shared energy that can be trusted and relied upon, passing from father to son." Miller adds: "Men may be seeking not only a closeness with their own fathers, but the generation of bonds with their own sons which allows them to fulfill roles of guidance and caretaking." Joe yearned to connect with his father more deeply, and he wanted a connection that was not just tied to sports or activities. He longed for opportunities to just sit down and talk about life with his dad.

Trying to make sense of the disconnect, Joe attributes it to his dad's stress from working hard to meet basic family needs and to be a provider and protector. Joe assumes his dad would often withdraw and spend time alone when he was home because he was carrying so much responsibility, as well as the stress of dealing with racism and discrimination in his job. After getting home from work, his dad would have dinner with the family, ask Joe about his homework, and then head down to the basement to watch TV, smoke a pipe, and listen to music.

Even as his dad withdrew from the family to be alone, Joe wanted a deeper connection. "I wanted to know what was on his mind, how he was feeling, what the fears or even the dreams were that he had for me and our family," Joe reflects now. "I was close with my dad in the sense that we *did* things together—but as I got older, I wanted deeper conversation that I hoped he would have initiated."

Joe took advantage of every opportunity to learn to know his dad as a person and not just as a provider. When friends would come over to visit his dad, Joe would find a place in the room where he could just sit and listen. Those moments gave him insight into who his dad was, and just being in the room listening and observing made Joe feel closer to his dad. Joe enjoyed those moments but always wanted to spend more time with his dad just to talk. What he desired most was to know his dad's heart, and to connect on an emotional level that would have strengthened their bond.

Living with a Complicated Dad

Joe's father had grown up in New Orleans during segregation. After graduating from high school, he joined the air force. During his time in the military, he would send money home to help his parents. His commitment to help the family freed up enough money for his oldest sister to attend college. Joe's father took pride in meeting the needs of his family.

When his time in the air force came to an end, he moved to New York and became an undercover narcotics agent for the US Treasury Department. "My dad was chasing gangsters. He was chasing drug dealers for the federal government," Joe tells me. "You get hardened because you don't know who you can talk to about anything because your life's on the line." As Joe explains the dangers and stresses of his dad's job, it's clear that he is still seeking to understand the reasons for his dad's distant behavior.

Joe's parents met while he was an undercover narcotics agent. One of his friends set them up on a blind date, and it wasn't long before they fell in love and got married. When Joe was born, his dad left his job as an undercover agent. The risks of leaving home and not making it back and of putting his family in danger were not worth it. His dad chose his family. Joe's dad never told Joe stories about his life undercover, although every now and then Joe's mom would sneak in a story to give him a glimpse into his dad's former life.

Joe's dad was a big man with an imposing physical stature that commanded respect. His voice was deep and would echo across a room. Joe respected and feared him. "My dad had a temper, and when he got mad you did not want to be around him," Joe remembers. "When Pops gets mad, he can clear out a house just by yelling. As I got older, I would see and hear that temper come out, and it pushed me away from him because I didn't want to do something to set him off."

Joe was thirteen when he started hearing his parents argue. Sometimes the arguments made Joe uncomfortable, and they intensified over the course of a few years. By the time he was preparing to leave for college, his parents were having more frequent conflicts, and he worried about what home would be like in his absence.

When Joe left for Rice University in Houston, where he played college basketball, the situation between his parents deteriorated significantly. Joe's closest friends knew about the troubles in his home and nicknamed him "The Peacemaker." "I was constantly breaking up arguments between my dad and my mom," he says. "It was not uncommon for me to get a phone call from home and have to hop in the car to break up an argument before someone got seriously hurt."

His parents eventually separated. Joe says he doesn't doubt that his dad loved his mom. For his dad, love and intimacy looked like being a provider, putting food on the table, and meeting family needs in practical ways. But for Joe, love would have looked like a peaceful home where his parents got along.

A Father's Anger

Throughout his childhood and into adult life, Joe longed for a more intimate, emotional connection with his dad. "I really didn't get to know him until two-and-a-half years prior to his unexpected death," Joe reflects now. His father had one heart attack shortly after separating from Joe's mom. His dad died of a massive second heart attack at age fifty-six. Joe shared with me that he had only witnessed his dad cry once, and that was when his father's mother came to stay with the family. Doctors discovered that she had a brain tumor, and the family was deeply concerned about her prognosis. When the family received the diagnosis, Joe recalled walking into the kitchen and seeing his dad leaning against a counter with his head bowed in silence. Joe walked in and hugged him. As they stood there holding each other in silence, his dad began to cry. "My dad taught me something in that moment that I still repeat at every funeral I do," Joe says. "My dad said, 'Son, death is a part of life. You must under-stand death if you're going to understand life.' I later understood his words through the lens of faith: the belief that if you have faith in Jesus Christ, death is not the end."

Growing up, Joe lacked for nothing. His father was a pro-vider. There was never a concern for the necessities of life, and his dad made sure that he received a quality education. But pro-vision and love are not the same thing. Parents provide out of love, but love has many expressions. For Joe, more complete expressions of love would have combined provision with greater peace at home. The two together would have made it a more emotionally safe space.

The absence of a peaceful home created a disconnect between Joe and his dad. The absence of peace between his parents denied Joe the opportunity to get to know his dad on a deeper emotional level. When his dad got angry, Joe felt intim-idated and afraid. When his dad got angry, it was better to just stay out of the way. Joe has vivid memories of those moments of his father's anger. But he wishes there were more memories of verbal expressions of love. "Pops loved me deeply, and told me as much from time to time. I always knew my dad loved me, with-out question. As I reflect back, I wish there were more opportu-nities to hear him say it," he says.

Hearing his dad say "I love you" more often would have given Joe the intimate relationship that he always wanted. Seeing a softer side of his dad would have drawn them even closer because it would have allowed Joe to see a softer side of him as a man. Joe's dad came from a generation of men who did not allow anyone, even their own sons, to witness their vulnerabili-ties. They believed that they had to convey a message of strength at all times. His dad grew up believing that crying was a sign of weakness.

I know a lot of Black men who grew up with fathers like Joe's. Just about all of them attribute the disconnected relationships with their fathers to the pressures and dangers their fathers experienced during segregation. Meeting the needs of their families while also modeling for their sons what would be required of them emotionally to survive in a segregated society—these labors required a particular, arguably numb, posture in the world.

What many of these fathers failed to understand is that their sons clearly saw their strength and would not have interpreted crying as weakness. Crying would have been evidence for the sons that their dads were capable of feeling something other than anger. When a young man shares in his dad's sadness and fears, their connection tends to deepen, and the son learns how to be a more emotionally healthy and strong man.

"If my dad were more emotionally vulnerable at times, it would have drawn me closer," Joe says. "If he said I love you more often and allowed me to see him during his vulnerable moments, it would have taught me that it's okay to let your guard down with the people who love and need to feel loved by you. I needed him to take the armor off sometimes."

We sit in silence for a while, thinking. "To this day I wish I could have had a deeper connection, and to this day I am very intentional about nurturing that connection between me and my son," Joe says. "I worked hard to let my son in so that we have a deeper emotional connection, because I don't want him to miss out on what I yearned to experience from my father."

When the Armor Comes Off

Joe's dad retired and his parents separated one year after Joe got married to his wife, Madelyn. His father resettled in California and ended up living with his dad, Joe's grandfather. Joe and his dad didn't talk for almost a month after he moved. Two months after their first conversation, his dad had his first heart attack. Joe flew to see him and stayed with him through his first heart procedure. Sitting at his dad's side the day before the surgery, Joe held his father's hand and told him that he would not leave his side until he knew that everything was going to be okay. Clasping Joe's hand firmly, his dad thanked him and said that he loved him.

That was one of the few times in Joe's life that he heard those words from his father. Verbal expressions of love should not have to wait for potential tragedies to occur. Giving voice to the language of love is something all of us need. It gives us strength during the good times and especially during the difficult ones.

Over the next two-and-a-half years, Joe and his dad began a new father-and-son journey together—one that was deeper, more emotional, and even spiritual, as Joe describes it. Joe was present for his dad, and they spent time talking about life, manhood, and family, and for Joe those interactions felt more like the peace and family he had always wanted. The armor had finally come off.

"Those were some of the best years of my life, those two-and-a-half years," Joe reflects. "He went from being a father to my best friend and I've told people this. He was always a father, but now he was a best friend. I wish the armor had come off sooner."

During the time Madelyn was preparing to give birth to their daughter, Joe called his dad and told him that he needed him to be with him for that moment. His dad agreed. He flew to Maryland and stayed for three weeks after his granddaughter was born.

Joe smiles the entire time that he tells the story. "To this day I remember him knocking on the door when he got in," he recalls. "He came to the door with a teddy bear in one arm and a fried turkey in his hands. He had the teddy bear for [Joia] and the fried turkey for us to eat as a family. He hung out with us."

Joe was getting the love he had always wanted from his dad. Over the course of those two-and-a-half years, Joe flew to California often so that they could spend time together. They talked, laughed, and had intimate conversations in which they shared fears, hopes, and dreams about life. Joe shows me a picture of his dad lying on the couch with his granddaughter on his chest as both of them slept. That time together would end up being the only time his dad would see any of Joe's children; four months later, his dad had the second heart attack and died.

Life had given Joe and his dad a second chance to be present for each other, develop deeper connections, and experience the kind of peaceful family environment that Joe had always longed for.

Takeaways

Joe's story speaks of a father who was present and who also had challenges with maintaining presence. Presence is a hospitable and welcoming emotional embrace that enables humans to know and be known. Like so many other Black men of his generation, Joe's father not only had to navigate the trauma of being reared in the Jim Crow South; he also had to traverse the terrain of the military and undercover law enforcement work. These organizations required Joe's father to isolate parts of himself. They are not institutions that lend themselves to cultivating emotional and psychological wholeness and living a fully integrated life. When one has to survive systematic and structural racism, it translates into all aspects of their life, especially the family system.

Joe experienced a father who was at times disconnected from his son. And unfortunately, Joe became the indirect recipient of harsh tones and argumentative disputes between his parents, which indicated to him to stay away. Anger is often a surface emotion and more accessible than emotions like sadness, disappointment, insecurity, depression, shame, and guilt.

In many households, high emotional reactivity and speaking harshly is commonplace. When parents expose children, even unintentionally, to this way of engaging, they internalize the behavior. They become isolated, and believe they need to bear the responsibility of being the mediator because they perceive their parents as lacking the capacity to do so.

Joe's narrative is a reminder to all men: emotional suppression only creates an unsafe emotional environment for themselves and their loved ones. His story also conveys the significance of men taking care of their traumatic and psychic wounds and diving deeply into the pain points of their experience. They need to heal old narratives so they can emerge with the power that comes from healing with intentionality. This is the type of love Joe's father needed in order to become more emotionally available for Joe and his mother.

CHAPTER 5

I WISH MY DAD LOVED HIMSELF MORE

MAX

During his teenage years, Max was not what anyone would define as a good kid. As the eldest of his dad's three sons, Max made some bad choices, and like many teenagers, he strayed from the path that his father had hoped he would follow. But even during those years, his father never lost hope that things would change, and he loved his son well during the most difficult of times.

It took several years, but eventually his dad got to experience the joy of seeing his son become a leader, loving husband, and proud father. Max eventually became a pastor and is currently the president and CEO of a Christian nonprofit. He and his wife, Dee Dee, have two children of their own: Jennifer, twenty-seven, and Joshua, twenty-four.

Max's dad is an example of what it looks like when unwavering love, hope, and relentless prayer pay off. He's the kind of dad every kid wants: a dad who doesn't give up and who loves you despite your mistakes.

Yet it's one thing to love your son through challenging times, look beyond his flaws, and believe in the man that you know he can become. It's another thing to offer yourself, as a father, that same kind of love.

Even a good father can feel like a failure. Max loves talking about his dad. He is proud of his father and has a great deal of respect for him. But if Max could have one wish come true for his dad, it would be this: that his dad could love himself as much as he loved everyone else.

A Devoted Dad

During his prime, Max's dad loved to have fun and was always the life of the party. Everyone liked him, and he could always get people to smile. The family were regular churchgoers. They were often the first to get there and always the last to leave because they had to wait until his dad was done hugging and chatting with everyone. Everyone in church knew him as a loving and kind-spirited man.

No one could ever question the amount of time and energy Max's dad invested in his three sons. He was all in and always present. "My father devoted his time and attention to me and my brothers in what I consider extraordinary ways," Max reflects now, as he sits in my home office and tells me his story.

Max's dad was the kind of father who made his home a safe and welcoming place for Max and his friends. Max's friends enjoyed the warmth of his dad's smile, and he was always happy to see them when they came over. The environment that his dad created in their home was a safe haven for his three sons' friends. Whenever friends were experiencing hard times, they would go to Max's house. A few friends from troubled homes even moved in with Max's family for extended periods of time, and his dad never turned them away.

Generosity and love were driving factors of his parents' hospitality. But letting his sons' friends hang out at the house or even move in, when necessary, also meant that Max's dad could be near his sons and keep an eye on them.

The more Max talks to me about his dad, the more impressed I become. From sports to fishing and camping, Max's dad did it all. He invested time with his sons. He believed in them, and he believed in their friends.

Max's dad didn't just sit on the sidelines; he got in the game. He was the scoutmaster when no one else wanted that role. He was the Little League baseball coach for the teams of kids that no one wanted to coach. Whatever it took to meet the needs of the kids is what Max's dad was willing to do. "He lived by the philosophy that, first and foremost, it was about everyone having a good time," Max says. "So he would play with every kid and he would treat everyone equally."

Max was on the wrestling team in high school. He attended a school that didn't have the financial resources to support their sports teams. As their season approached, Max and his teammates took it upon themselves to raise money for wrestling mats. After school and on weekends they stood on corners holding signs and coffee cans asking passersby to help their team. You've probably witnessed young athletes standing along a street in the rain, asking for help in support of their dreams. I have. More often than not, I feel compelled to share a few dollars with them because I know what it feels like to need the help of a stranger to pursue a dream.

But how often have you seen adults standing out with the kids, asking for money? That's where Max's dad comes in. He'd stand there with the student athletes, holding a sign or coffee can and asking if people would help his son and teammates.

When other parents couldn't be there, the kids could count on Max's dad. Sometimes he was the only adult there to cheer them on. "He was there at every match supporting us," says Max. "I was a horrible wrestler in my first two years. I can remember getting out on the mat and just getting destroyed. I would look up in the stands and my dad was there, and he would give me a thumbs-up. At one point I said, 'Dad, you do realize that I'm getting killed out there?' But my dad was always upbuilding and encouraging and positive." He was loved by the kids and respected by coaches.

But Max's dad's opinion of himself never measured up to his own expectations or dreams. His dad loved to dream big. Some would say that the effort he put into making those dreams come true didn't really measure up to the level of the dreams themselves. Lack of effort and self-doubt often keeps us from turning dreams into destiny.

Max's dad may not have possessed the skills to make his own dreams come true. Or perhaps he lacked the capacity to commit to making those dreams become reality. But when it came to being an engaged dad, he was a success.

What's a Father's Time Worth?

After listening to Max share story after story about his dad, I am surprised when he suddenly pauses. We sit in silence for a moment. It feels as if our silence is a way of expressing gratitude for his dad. Max leans forward, elbows on his lap, and clasps his hands. Max reaches for a tissue on the coffee table as he begins to cry. "I guess now I'm going to have to pay you for a therapy session," he jokes, and we laugh.

Fond memories of his dad bring back moments of both joy and sadness, Max says. When Max was in middle school, his dad started a routine of spending one night a week hanging out with each of his sons. For Max it was Wednesdays. After coming home from a day of work, he would say to Max, "Okay, let's go; it's Dad's night out," which meant he and Max would do something together unrelated to sports, school, or anything else. Their time together would vary. Sometimes it meant going out for a burger and fries. Sometimes they went fishing. Sometimes they'd grab a bag of quarters and head to the arcade to play pinball with Max's friends. His dad could hardly play the games, but he did it anyway. At times he would just feed quarters into the machines, step back, and smile as he watched Max play with his friends. He wasn't just creating great memories for his son; he was building a legacy that went on to have a profound impact for years to come.

So where is the sadness? "When he looks back on his life, I think he thinks of himself as a failure because he never became a great businessman," Max reflects. "I think he wonders if life might have turned out different for him if he had put his time into other things, like business." Max is silent for a moment. "In my mind, he chose well with his time. It could not have been easy for him, because he wasn't just doing it with me; he was doing it with both my brothers as well. For several years, he set aside one night a week for each of the three of us. So three nights a week he was devoting his free time completely to his kids."

Max sees the value in how his dad spent his time, and he wishes his dad could see that too. "It was the time he invested in us that has resulted in some significant value for my brothers, our friends, and me. I don't think my dad feels completely good about that, and that makes me sad. I have always wished that he could see the value of that part of his life."

Just a few years ago, Max was having dinner with his best friend from high school, Ted. Ted had a rough life growing up. His father didn't have much to do with him, and Ted frequently got into trouble. It bothered Max's dad that Max and Ted spent so much time together, but he allowed it. During dinner that night, Max and Ted reflected on their high school years, laughing and sharing memories. Suddenly, Ted turned serious. "I want to tell you something I never told you before," he said to Max. "I used to sit and just fantasize about what it would be like to be in a family like yours—in a family where parents actually cared about you and involved themselves in your life. I used to love to be places with your dad because I would just watch how he would engage with you and your brothers. I would think *that* is how fathers ought to be, and how mine never was like that."

Ted's family and Max's parents still live down the street from each other in the old neighborhood. Knowing his dad often feels like a failure when it comes to his working life, and how his dreams of striking it rich through one of his big ideas never came true, Max encouraged Ted to stop by the house next time he's in town to tell his dad the impact his presence had on Ted's life. Ted did just that.

Several months later, Max got a call from his dad. "You'll never believe what happened," his dad told him incredulously. "There was a knock on the door and Ted—do you remember Ted from when you were a kid? He came by the house and was telling me how much I meant to him when you guys were kids. I didn't even know the guy liked me!" Even after hearing about the positive impact he had on someone's life, Max's dad still found a way to see himself as less than how others see him.

When Max talks about his dad, his greatest wish is that he would love himself with the same degree of acceptance and forgiveness that he readily made available to others. Even though he has a master's degree, taught at a university, and designed homes for celebrities, he would still describe himself to others as "a short, fat little hillbilly." He couldn't see himself as being worthy, even while he wanted other people to know that *they* were. His deeds and words of encouragement continue to have a lasting impact on those who have been fortunate enough to know him.

Letters of Encouragement, Prayers of Hope

Max's dad didn't say "I love you" very often, but he expressed his love through letters, which he wrote often. "At multiple points as I was growing up, my dad would write letters to me where he would express a lot of things and he would put in writing the depths of his love," Max tells me. He picked up the habit of writing letters from his own dad, Max's grandfather. Max's grandfather wrote to a different person every single night of his adult life to encourage them. At Max's grandfather's funeral, people came from neighboring cities and states carrying the letters they had received over the years. Some of them had saved the letters for thirty or forty years.

Max's dad continued that tradition of kindness with his own sons. Those letters from his dad had a profound impact on Max's life. Max saves the letters that he has received from his dad in a box. "The times that I received those letters that were the most meaningful to me were actually during the years of some of my worst rebellions," he reflects now. When he left home after graduating from high school, Max's behavior continued to spiral down. Even then his dad continued to write him letters of encouragement. "I can remember on multiple occasions when I would receive letters from my dad, and they were almost always out of the blue."

Even during those rebellious years, his dad would write and tell Max that he was proud of him. It meant a lot to Max to read those words, and as I listen to him talk now, it's clear that they still mean a lot to him. When Max began to turn the corner, finding his way back to living the values instilled in him by his dad, he had a significant faith experience. Although he doesn't go into detail, he describes it as a moment that transformed his life. Several months after that experience of God's love and forgiveness, he went back home. One day he decided to visit the church in which he grew up and where his parents were still members. It's the same church where they would be the last to leave as they waited for his dad to hug everyone before going home.

As he walked through the church, Max was approached by a man who was a friend of his father's. The man looked Max in the eyes, smiled, and put his arm around his shoulder. "I knew you would be back," the man said.

Not fully understanding what the man meant, Max replied, "Back home?"

"No, I knew you would be back to the right path and to faith and to getting your life together, because I am in a group of four men who meet with your father every week," he told Max. "I have watched every week for the last several years as your father has knelt down in front of a folding chair and wept in prayer until there were just pools of tears on the chair."

As Max shares that story with me, he begins to cry—not about what his dad's friend was saying to him but what his dad had been saying to God on his behalf when he knelt down in front of that chair. "Knowing the depths of my father's faith, I don't doubt that his prayers had an impact on how my life has turned out," Max says.

At the time that Max comes over to my home to talk about his dad, his father's eighty-eighth birthday is just a few months away. His health is declining, and rapidly advancing dementia minimizes his short-term memories. Max has been trying to figure out some way to honor his dad that, despite his mental state, will help him feel valued. After reflecting on his dad's journey and the impact he has had on so many lives over the years, Max decides to reach out to some of those people to collect their stories and offer them as gifts to his dad. I can see the joy in his eyes as he ponders the possibility and begins to smile.

Takeaways

Max's "I Wish My Dad" story is warm, inspiring, and loving. It takes us on a journey of understanding the impact a father's intentional presence and investment can have, not only on their children but also on their children's friends. It is a reminder that what we may assume is insignificant because "that's just what we're supposed to do" can be paramount in the lives of others. Max experienced an unconditional love from his father that was not determined by his morality or good performance. His father's unconditional love was connected to his humanity and his father's ability to see the intrinsic value within him. May we all be loved in ways that propel us toward our highest good and best selves.

Max's story also invites us to consider how fatherhood can be tied to the toxic expectations surrounding masculinity: productivity, wealth, career success. This often stimulates insecurity, diminishes self-esteem, and arouses depression in fathers, which keeps them from seeing themselves fully.

This limiting lens of masculinity meant Max's father was unable to acknowledge and affirm his own success as a man and father connected to the thriving of his sons and their friends, which is immeasurable. Even as he felt bad about himself, Max's father created a legacy of emotional intelligence and wellness that will continue to sustain present and future generations.

This is a lesson for every father to consider: do not forgo loving yourself as you extend love to your children.

CHAPTER 6

I WISH MY DAD TOOK CARE OF HIMSELF

DANIEL

Daniel and I have been friends for fifteen years. We met when I owned a public relations consulting company in Washington, DC, and he held senior leadership positions with several of my clients over the years. He and I traveled the country for meetings and became fast friends. Daniel is a good man in every way. In business he leads with integrity, and his values undergird solid decisions and partnerships. Daniel cares about doing good in the world with measurable impact. He cares about people and about the issues that impact the most vulnerable populations.

Daniel, who is fifty years old, is married, and is the proud father of three children—aged fourteen, twelve, and ten. He is a vice president at a foundation that supports research in religion and science. He is always thinking about and planning the future for his family. He assesses the long-term value of selling a home versus renting it out. He chooses the best companies in the stock market for long-term growth that ensure his family will be okay when he retires.

Now, listening to his story, I understand why.

A Leader Who Cared

Daniel was five years old when his father died from a cerebral hemorrhage. He had walked to his car after work and collapsed when he sat down in the driver's seat. Daniel's father was overweight, smoked three packs of cigarettes a day, and generally did not take care of himself. He was only fifty-two.

What he knows about his father is mostly through stories he has heard and the limited memories from when he was a young child. Daniel's dad was both brilliant and charismatic. People came to him for help often. He was a visionary leader who was very involved in his community and politics. Publicly, he was highly respected, but behind the scenes he had his own challenges.

Daniel's dad was an attorney who fought for the people of the city of Utica, New York, and maintained his integrity even when others succumbed to the corruption that surrounded them. In the end, emotionally devastated by the outcomes, his dad moved on from his engagement with politics and into the private sector. He loved the city of Utica, but he never fully recovered from the impact of the corrupt powers that were ruining the lives of people in his community. Daniel thinks the stress of navigating the political powers of his beloved city contributed to his decline in health and eventual death.

"My dad was betrayed by the power structure, and his name was slandered," Daniel says. The family moved to Connecticut around the time Daniel was born. "He would go back from Connecticut to Utica on the weekends to see his friends," Daniel recalls. "His friends were still working and planning and trying to do things in the city, and he just wasn't a part of it anymore." Daniel pauses, thinking about the weight of stress and sadness his father carried. "I think that just killed him."

Daniel didn't have his dad for very long, but he knew that his father loved him. "He adored me, and I think the confidence I carry with me in my life is because I knew I was loved without a doubt." Daniel has few memories of time with his dad. He recalled moments when they walked to a candy store or when he would ride with him in his convertible with the top down. He recalled a visit to Disney World and memories of walking around the theme park with his dad. There were also the tender moments of playing with him in the garden behind his grandparents' house. His dad was present and attentive. Several times during our conversation, Daniel points out memories of his dad holding his hand. The connection of his father's touch made him feel cared for and close to his dad.

"I remember he would come home from work when we lived in Connecticut. Like a lot of men of his time, he worked late. He worked until eight or nine o'clock at night and he would come home. He was an old-fashioned guy; there was supposed to be food ready when he came home. If it wasn't meat, it wasn't food. I remember him putting me on his knee and feeding me little pieces of steak."

Holding hands as they walked together, playing in his grandmother's garden, sitting on his father's knee as his dad fed him: it's easy to understand why Daniel knew very early in his life that he was loved and adored by his dad.

Cultural Differences

Daniel's grandparents had immigrated to New York from Lebanon in the 1910s. They were immigrants with very little education who would later have three sons. One of their sons, Daniel's dad, later went to Harvard Law School on a scholarship. Another of their sons was a Rhodes Scholar, and another son got two master's degrees.

When Daniel's dad was seventeen, he got a job in the office of the cement factory where his father worked as the foreman. The owner of the company told Daniel's dad that after he graduated from high school, he could come back and work at the company full time. Daniel's dad respectfully declined the offer and told the owner that he was going to college. The owner told Daniel's dad that he should be proud to take the job offer because, unlike his father, who had to work with his hands as the foreman, Daniel's dad would be able to work with his mind and be paid well for it. But Daniel's father turned down the job again and said he was going to college. And he did.

Daniel's dad was studying for his undergraduate degree when World War II interrupted. He, like so many other men of his generation, enlisted soon after the bombing of Pearl Harbor—in Daniel's dad's case, the next day. He fought in the Pacific Theater before returning from the war and finished up his college degree.

After graduating from college, he was trying to figure out what he was going to do next. One morning, his cousin was going to Syracuse to take a college entrance exam and asked Daniel's dad to give him a ride. "The story goes that my dad said, 'Sure, I'll give you a ride,' and took him over to Syracuse and dropped him off. Apparently, on the same day, at the same time, they were offering the LSAT—the entrance exam for law school. So my dad decided, *What the hell; I'll just go and take it*. He sat down and took the LSAT . . . and got a scholarship offer from Harvard." No test prep, no planning; he just took the test and got a scholarship.

Daniel's father and mother had been introduced to each other by mutual friends. His mom was of Italian, Irish, and French descent, and she was divorced. His dad knew his mother would not approve of him being in a relationship with a woman who was not Lebanese and who had been previously married.

So Daniel's father hid the relationship with Daniel's mother from his family. They ended up having a child together (Daniel's older brother), and he hid that fact from his family too—for ten full years. When Daniel tells me this, it takes a while to sink in. Daniel's grandparents didn't know about his brother's existence for a decade.

His parents placed a high value on maintaining Lebanese tradition. Daniel's father checked off all the necessary boxes to meet the expectations of his parents—until he fell in love with Daniel's mother. This became a great internal schism for Daniel's father, so much so that he participated in the erasure of his marriage and firstborn child for ten years.

Our secrets have a way of revisiting us. What we perceive as mistakes are connected to shame and guilt. Daniel's father kept this secret for fear of disappointing his mother and being ostracized by his family. "My mother told plenty of stories about how she lived on hot dogs for weeks before I was born because that was all she could afford and she needed to feed my brother. She had to wash my brother's clothes by hand in the bathtub because there was no money for a washing machine," Daniel reflects. "My dad didn't take care of her. Then when I was born, he kind of swooped in and tried harder to accept his responsibilities and to be the dad."

Just five years later, Daniel's dad died suddenly. Daniel was just a little boy, and his brother was fifteen. Daniel's brother ended up struggling with drugs most of his life and died when he was just forty-one. "I don't know the exact cause of death," Daniel says. "But thank God he lived long enough to have a successful career and have a wonderful relationship with the mother of his children. His kids are amazing, and I adore them. But his death was just another tragedy. I have outlived my brother. I have nearly outlived my dad."

Daniel's father loved a woman he didn't think his family could accept, a woman who had her own story. She was the woman who gave birth to his children, and the woman he had chosen to marry. Daniel wishes his dad could have been vulnerable to love. Love could have given him the courage to confront challenges and choose his family above all else. "I think if he had been more vulnerable to love, he would have been more willing to be open to the family he had," Daniel says. "Being more open to the family he had would have allowed him to accept them." If love had been the guiding force for Daniel's dad, there would have been no challenge he wasn't willing to face for the sake of his family. "If my dad had been more vulnerable to love, he would have been willing to take on the challenge of his parents and say, *This is the relationship I'm in. This is the life I'm in.*"

Loving in the way that Daniel described would have had a life-changing impact on Daniel's mom and brother. His dad had a lot of love for people in their community. Daniel's mom shared stories with him of how his dad used to give away a great deal of his work to people who needed his help. People would show up on his dad's doorstep looking for free legal advice; he would give them his time and expertise. "At least for the first ten years, my dad didn't make those same sacrifices for his family," Daniel reflects. "It seems like he threw up walls and barriers to protect himself from feeling and being honest with himself and other people about who he was."

Daniel's father wrestled with the opinions of others, the tension of cultural differences, and the opinions of his own parents. He wasn't able to overcome those conflicts within himself in order to choose his family.

Prioritizing Health as an Act of Love

While Daniel felt his father's love, he wishes that a love for his family could have guided his dad's choices, especially his choices about his own health. "I wish that he would have loved us enough to take care of himself and said, 'I want to be here for my family so that I can take care of them,'" Daniel reflects.

When his dad came back from the war, like many men of that era, he smoked heavily. He had an unhealthy diet, gained a lot of weight, and put himself at risk for an untimely death. His dad was very focused, but his priorities were in the wrong order. He was focused on himself and what others thought: his career success, his personal goals, and what he was trying to achieve in life. "I think for the first ten years my mother and brother were not his primary focus," Daniel reflects. "I wish he had really thought through the question: *How am I going to live up to this responsibility—not just in terms of how much money I make but making sure I'm still here?*"

Toward the end of his life, Daniel's father began to see what he had missed by not making his wife and children his priority. When the family moved away from Utica and relocated to Connecticut, Daniel says, it represented the start of his life with his family. Unfortunately, it didn't last very long, as he passed away just five years later.

"If my dad had cared for his health, he might very well have been here to help give me some guidance on how to navigate the world," Daniel reflects. "I had to figure it out without him. My mom and my brother needed him to be here—all of us needed him. Caring for his health would have been an act of love that all of us would have benefited from."

Daniel only had five years with his dad, but in listening to him share about his father, I can tell he has inherited many of his father's positive traits. Like his dad, Daniel is generous and truly cares about helping people. Over the course of his career, he has fought for workers' rights, and has been involved in political campaigns, working for candidates who value the well-being of all people. These were the things his dad cared about too.

His father's way of showing affection through how he spent time with Daniel, holding his hand and sharing tender moments, is also a part of the legacy of love that Daniel now offers his children. No parent is perfect, but Daniel is pretty amazing. He does his best to love his own children in unique ways based on their personalities: hopping with one daughter, playing sports with another, wrestling or doing pull-ups with his son, and lying down with them in the evening at bedtime.

"Family is the most important thing to me, and certainly that had to be impacted by the fact that mine was so broken early on,"

Daniel says. "I want to create a stable, loving environment for my kids, and I want my work to be important. But at the end of the day, if all I do in my life is raise three functioning adults who can contribute to the world around them? Well, that's good."

Knowing the impact that lack of physical health and poor choices around wellness had on his own family, Daniel takes care of himself as an act of love. "Because death has come so frequently and suddenly into my life on multiple occasions, I have a really keen sense of time," Daniel tells me. "Every time my children leave the house, I think, *This could be the last time I will ever see them*. That's a part of why I kiss them every morning before they leave for school."

Takeaways

Daniel's "I Wish My Dad" story carries the complexity of identity, the burden of secrets, and the impact of a father's early death on a family system. Daniel's father belonged to a generation of men who were expected to bear the weight of their emotional pain in isolation. Most of those men didn't realize the detrimental emotional and physical effects such an approach could have on their overall well-being.

Daniel's father also developed a capacity for holding secrets well. Secrets can cause stress on our emotional lives *and* in our bodies.

Daniel's father may have also been exposed to horrors while serving in World War II. If so, he likely also held those stories as secrets. An adage popular in addiction recovery circles—*we are only as sick as our secrets*—holds true for Daniel's father in light of his heavy drinking and smoking and poor diet, which culminated in an untimely death.

Daniel's father's work ethic may have also been rooted in overcompensating for insecurity with his identity as a Lebanese man with an Irish-Italian spouse and children who were multiethnic. He may have perceived his identity as a visionary political leader within his Utica community as the only thing he excelled in. If this was the core identity he valued, having this identity implode as a result of slander and betrayal and corruption was utterly devastating. Daniel's statement is appropriate: "I think that just killed him."

Daniel's father clearly struggled with self-love. What men believe about who they are informs the ways in which they treat themselves and the people they love. How could Daniel's father provide a vulnerable love to his wife and sons when he did not offer that love to himself? Daniel's story is an invitation to all men who are leading and loving from their secrets and from their fears: learn to unburden yourself. This unburdening could happen in a therapist's office, with a pastor or other spiritual leader, or as part of an intentional group dedicated to supporting men in healing.

Daniel now honors his father's life and legacy by loving his family through prioritizing his health. Men, you are worth your wholeness and worthy of healing.

CHAPTER 7

I WISH MY DAD DIDN'T ASSERT HIS MASCULINITY

HODARI

Hodari is the definition of a loyal and caring friend. Over the years I've witnessed how he shows up for people, celebrating with them when life is good and simply being present during the challenging times. During the pandemic I watched him visit people in the hospital, travel for funerals, and schedule regular socially distanced meetups so that friends could get together for drinks and a few laughs. Being around Hodari has given me a deeper appreciation for friendships and the way in which maintaining them requires intentionality.

Hodari is a Presbyterian pastor who lives with his wife and family in Atlanta. He is very involved in the lives of his two young sons. As any good dad does, Hodari loves his sons, but I think he also admires them. Listening to him have conversations with his oldest, Asad, who is nine, I can tell Hodari is both father and friend to him. Asad is wise for his age, and he and Hodari talk about all kinds of things: politics, life, movies, emotions. Asad shares his feelings with his dad, and Hodari creates a safe space for him to do so without judgment or shame. I've seen many dads teach their sons to only be "strong men," as defined by culture, not realizing that expressing feelings leads to true strength and emotional balance.

Hodari learned a lot about being a dad from his own father. The lessons come from looking back at his childhood and learning what worked and what did not. He is very mindful of what he needed from his dad and what would have allowed him to thrive. He can identify what was good, what he wishes had been different, and what would have allowed their relationship to grow.

A Dad's "Wifely Duties" and the Pressure to Succeed

Hodari's dad might be described as "a man's man": firm, tough, and physically imposing. In the home he was a very affectionate father, a consistent presence. But he was also very domineering. It was a my-way-or-the-highway kind of environment—perhaps not all the time, but most of the time.

Hodari's dad's work schedule allowed him to be home during the day. As a result, he played a different role in the home life of his children from what many dads do. When Hodari starts telling me about his dad's role in the home, I can tell he has some concerns about how his dad viewed his own role. "He referred to the daily tasks as his 'wifely duties,'" Hodari tells me, looking down in discouragement for a moment. "He felt his masculinity was challenged because he had to do certain things my mother couldn't do because her job was more demanding. He cooked. He washed clothes. He made sure we were off to school. He was there in the evening. He was going to different events at our schools." Hodari's dad attended PTA meetings and did other things that he deemed to be women's responsibilities. He would joke about and laugh off his role, but Hodari could tell his dad felt that it threatened his masculinity. Men with traditional backgrounds often see such tasks as "women's work"—when in reality they have nothing to do with gender and everything to do with parenting.

Hodari's dad may have been uncomfortable with doing tasks he perceived as women's work, but those very tasks also allowed him to be engaged in the lives of his children. Hodari's mom, the breadwinner in the family, commuted to New York from their home in New Jersey. Hodari's dad was home during the day and able to take care of the kids while his wife was at work. Hodari's father had a hard time accepting that his wife made more money than he did. His challenge was finding a way to see that making less money had nothing to do with being a good father or a good man. "Most of his friends in our neighborhood made the money in their households," Hodari says. "I think my father was probably the only one whose wife garnered a salary well above his, and he wrestled with that."

Hodari now holds a healthy idea of manhood, one that he wishes his father could have embraced. "I wish my dad had understood the value in sharing the responsibility," he says. "I wish he hadn't tried to assert his masculinity with my mother." Hodari's dad did things to make himself feel like he was maintaining his position as a man within the household. For years his mother never drove a car, and his dad drove her everywhere. "She wanted to get her license," Hodari tells me. "She wanted that sense of independence, and it just never happened." That was his father's way of exhibiting some sense of control. He drove her to and from work and to the train station for her daily commute. "I wish he had valued the teamwork that came with co-laboring with my mother. I wish he could have understood that his responsibility was just as important as hers and what he was doing with us was just as valuable. I don't think he ever grasped that, even up until his death; he simply did not see the value of his role and how important it was for us."

Hodari's dad lived vicariously through his children, pushing them hard to achieve the social and economic success that he was unable to achieve himself. The pressure he placed on his children came at a high price. "My father's tactics were abusive in the sense that disobedience came with harsh penalties, such as beatings and manual labor," Hodari remembers. "I remember one year moving logs from one side of the yard to the other—for what reason I don't know, other than I had received a C in a class. I remember vividly my dad causing my brother to get left back a quarter in eighth grade because he had two Bs on his report card. He had one full semester to make that up, and then he made the honor roll. After that my father let him go to the ninth grade."

The pressure affected each of Hodari's siblings differently. Hodari shared that he often struggled with a sense of not meeting his dad's standards. Nothing ever seemed like it was enough. Hodari knew this wasn't healthy and, as an adult, has stopped chasing his dad's approval or trying to live up to his expectations. "I have become comfortable with who I am," he says. "I've had to affirm myself and be proud of myself for my accomplishments. But for many years, even after my dad died, I held on to the mental pressure of trying to live up to his expectations and wondering if it was ever enough."

Receiving Affection from a "Manly Man"

I am curious to learn more about what Hodari means by his dad being a "manly man." He shares that his dad's generation considered a man's man to be a tough guy who isn't a pushover and who doesn't back down. Hodari's dad was a Golden Gloves boxing champ and spent numerous years studying martial arts. "Today we would call it hypermasculinity," Hodari says. "Whatever you call it, he engaged in that bravado, that behavior."

Many cultural ideals of manhood don't include being emotionally healthy. It's as if physical strength and emotional toughness are signs that a man can protect the family from danger and not be taken advantage of—yet these ideas about strength can just as easily leave men emotionally unavailable and distant. But in talking to men about their fathers—and in watching fathers like Hodari with their own children—I see so clearly that what children need to become emotionally healthy and balanced is a father who makes them feel emotionally safe enough to express their feelings.

When I ask Hodari to tell me about what love from his dad looked like, he pauses for a moment. "He came from that generation where a child just didn't have an opinion," he says. "That approach left me feeling as if I wasn't valued. I wish he had understood that aspect of love that requires valuing and listening to others—even if they are children."

Hodari's dad was firm, intimidating, and demanding, but at the same time he was great with affection and compassionate touch. His dad wasn't afraid to embrace Hodari. When he was upset, Hodari found great value in receiving a comforting hug from his dad. "He didn't mind holding us," Hodari remembers. "If I did something like fall and scrape my knee, he'd pick me up and comfort me. That's the kind of person he was."

Hodari smiles when he talks about receiving hugs from his dad. Such memories clearly bring back warm feelings. "Every night before we went to bed, my dad would end the night with a kiss on the cheek, then say, 'I love you,'" Hodari recalls. "That's something I continue even today with my boys. I tell them, 'I love you. You're the greatest. You're a genius,' and then I turn the lights out and leave the room."

Trauma, Toughness, and Health

Growing up, Hodari didn't understand why his dad was so tough on him and his siblings. Years after his father died, Hodari learned that when his father was a teenager, his father's uncle had almost sexually assaulted him. The uncle moved across the country, and for years Hodari didn't even know about this uncle. He learned the story and the impact that it had on his father from his grandmother.

Hodari connects his father's hypermasculine persona partly with the trauma of that experience. "I wish men in my dad's generation had gone to therapy," he says. "If he had gone to therapy, he could have worked through all the issues connected to the situation with his uncle. If he had done his emotional healing work, he would not have behaved the way he did with me and my brothers."

As Hodari reflects on the kind of man his dad was, he sees a connection between that hypermasculinity and health. "I think not seeing a doctor when he wasn't feeling well or receiving regular checkups came from that belief: *I'm a man, and I am invincible*." Hodari's dad's death was premature and avoidable, and his passing was the result of some bad decisions regarding his health. His decline in health started with what appeared to be a common cold. Thinking it was minor, his father chose not to see a doctor. The symptoms persisted, though, and when he finally went to see a doctor, he was diagnosed with a virus that had attacked the walls of his heart. "He had thought he could handle it on his own," Hodari says. "But he couldn't. As a result, my younger siblings and I were left without a father for our teenage years and on." I sense the tension and anger Hodari feels as he thinks about the fact that his father might still be alive if he had valued his own health more. He still misses his dad, and he feels like he lost him too soon.

Hodari's dad also made some business decisions that did not take into consideration his personal health or a long-term view of the family's financial future. After learning of his diagnosis, Hodari's dad started a business, and he sold his life insurance policy to obtain startup money for a business. Even after his diagnosis, when the doctor told him he had only a few years to live, he still wasn't thinking about his health. In the end, that choice would have a detrimental effect on the family. "When he passed, we went from living like middle-class folk to just barely making it—poverty," Hodari says. "When my mother took ill, it got even worse. I held a lot of resentment and anger around his inability to be forward-thinking about decisions or to take into consideration how he could secure a future for all of us."

Because of his father's choices, life was hard for Hodari and his siblings as they were growing up. His death had a devastating impact both emotionally and financially. "I wish I had had more time with him," Hodari says. "At every major event and juncture, I always reflect about what it would be like if he were here: from the time I got married, to the time I bought my first home, to the birth of my children. That question is always there when those things happen: *I wonder what it would be like if my father were here?*"

Doing Things Differently

Hodari has taken the lessons he learned from his dad's choices and applied them to his own health. Mindful of how important his presence is to his wife and two children, he gets regular physicals and sees a cardiologist because of a family history of heart disease. He started getting colonoscopies and prostate screenings before age forty. He also plans and invests with a long-term view that takes into consideration the needs of his family both now and in the future. He wants to make sure they will always be able to thrive without the stress of economic instability.

Hodari gained a lot of wisdom from reflecting on his childhood experiences and the examples set by his dad. Remembering how present his father was and the value of it growing up, Hodari finds creative ways to stay connected with his sons, Asad and Asim. As the pastor of a prominent and thriving congregation in the Atlanta area, Hodari oversees numerous community impact building projects in addition to traditional aspects of church: visiting parishioners for prayer, leading Bible studies, and preaching on Sunday mornings. Asad, his older son, loves going to work with him when he can.

When it comes to meeting the emotional needs of his sons, Hodari is mindful that he needs to be gentle. "There are times where I try to make them recover too fast and not engage them in what they are feeling," he says with regret. "I've learned that there are ways in which experiences with my dad show up in good and bad ways. I work hard to let the good things I got from him come forward in how I love my boys."

Asim, who was less than one year old at the time of our interview, cries a lot. "Sometimes it's hard, because my trigger from the negative parts of my dad is to see crying as a sign of weakness," he says. "But then I remember that's what babies do. That's their language. I'm learning to be more patient and under-standing. That is how he communicates right now. At ten months he can't talk. If he is hungry, he is going to cry. If he is uncom-fortable, he is going to cry." Hodari tells me he is learning not to force his sons out of developmental stages.

Like Hodari says, he works hard to bring forward the good things his father gave him while letting go of the harmful mes-sages. Hodari's father may not have always felt that he lived up to his own expectations, but the value of his presence was priceless. Hodari has gleaned the best parts of who his dad was and incor-porates them into how he loves his children. "I think my boys will be happy with the choices I make about time because I value them more than anything else," Hodari says. "In terms of being visible, whether it is at my son's school events, or being with him at his sporting events: I will leave church meetings and board meetings—even if they are not over—to be where my sons are, because I just value the time."

For Hodari, the time that he spends with his sons is not "women's work" or a threat to his masculinity; time and invest-ment in his sons' lives are simply what love looks like.

Takeaways

Hodari's "I Wish My Dad" story speaks of the fragility of a masculinity built on rigid gender roles. Healthy masculinity means owning and acknowledging the feminine energy that men possess and must access to live a life of wellness. It is the feminine energy within us that nurtures, expresses, creates, and senses. It is this energy that Hodari operates in when making sure his health is in optimal condition. Hodari's father was accessing this part of his humanity, albeit begrudgingly, when he was fulfilling his "wifely duties."

Hodari's father's fragile masculinity was also layered with the trauma of almost being sexually assaulted by his uncle. This unhealed wound showed up in how he engaged his sons with directives that limited the full expression of their humanity as children.

If Hodari's father had been taught that sensitivity and nurturing qualities are not emasculating, but instead signs of strength and emotional wellness, his father may have not led with his insecurities, which turned into dominance. He may have been able to see the immense value he brought to his sons, marital partnership, and overall household. He may have been less controlling, or not controlling at all, with his wife. He may have understood that an assertion of power was unnecessary because he would have been operating powerfully as a nurturing presence and in the fullness of his humanity.

Men, you deserve to no longer deny your feminine energy. Nurture yourself by allowing someone to journey with you as you confront the pain points of your experience. This will strengthen the power within you. Therapy, life coaching, spiritual direction, alternative therapies, meditation, prayer rituals, and other healing modalities are available to you. You are worth your wholeness.

CHAPTER 8

I WISH MY DAD GAVE ME HIS ATTENTION

KEVIN

The applause and accolades of others provide a temporary emotional high for many men. But seeking external validation can never really fill the void of what they wanted but never received from their dads.

As Kevin sits across from me in my office for the interview, I can see in his eyes that he still carries the sadness of wanting his dad to see him, notice him, and be proud. Kevin, a musician and author in his forties, is a very kind and compassionate person. He's a family man who loves his wife and three children. If you were to sit down with him for a conversation over a cup of coffee, it wouldn't take long to realize that he's one of those special people who is genuinely interested in what you have to say. Conversations with Kevin have depth. He and I have talked about everything from faith to beating self-doubt to overcoming the performance trap.

Throughout our conversation, I learn the rest of his story. He never felt like he received his father's attention, and it left a void in him. To fill that void, Kevin's need for approval grew to the extent that he'd seek approval from *anyone*. "It sounds pitiful when I say it," he says sheepishly, "but I realize that there's still this little boy in me thinking I have to prove myself somehow."

I can also tell that this isn't the first time Kevin has reflected on these issues. Making sense of his father's emotional distance and approach to life has troubled him for a while. Kevin doesn't know my questions in advance, but his answers are well-thought-out per M-W. It's clear that he is ready to figure out how his longing for his father's approval is connected to his lifelong search for approval and validation, attention, and love.

Admiring an Emotionally Distant Dad

Kevin loves his father, admired him, and always desired a close relationship. "I was always trying to get his attention, trying to say *Hey, I'm here!*" he tells me. "It never seemed to work. He always seemed lost in his own world."

For most of Kevin's childhood and into his adult life, his dad was emotionally unavailable and, for a stretch of time, physically absent. His father was always gone. "He drank a lot when I was young," he reflects. "He seemed selfish to me because I felt like he was never there for us."

Outside of their home, his father was a different man, open and friendly. In fact, many would call him a local celebrity. He's a Hall of Fame pool player in the billiards world, and around town when Kevin was growing up, he was always a big deal. He was a baseball umpire in the community, organizing tournaments for adults, as well as a professional bowler. Kevin's dad always had people's attention because of his talents. "Wherever we went, people always stopped my dad to say hi," Kevin remembers. "It didn't matter where we were; someone always wanted to talk to him. I really wanted that same attention."

Kevin was eight years old when he started going around town with his dad—but it wasn't because his dad took Kevin with him. Kevin simply followed his dad everywhere he went. If his dad had his umpire stuff on, he knew to follow his dad to the baseball park. If he had his pool cue with him, Kevin knew that he'd be following his dad to the pool hall. His dad walked to most places he was going, so when he left the house, Kevin just followed him.

Kevin was proud of his dad's accomplishments, but the things that everyone loved his dad for were the same things that he never shared with Kevin. "He was always so busy doing these things, but really not with me and my brother," he says. Oddly enough, though, Kevin became a good pool player because he had followed his dad to different pool halls and watched him beat everyone he played against. Kevin learned the game on his own and, like most things in his life, he became excellent at it, just like his dad.

"I admired the fact that so many people admired him." Kevin was proud of his dad because he was good at what he did, and because he was able to make people appreciate both his talent and personality. But there was a lot of confusion around those feelings. On the one hand, he admired his dad and wanted to be around him. At the same time, Kevin felt like he was on the outside, looking in at his dad's life. He was standing on the sidelines of his father's life, watching. Instead of feeling the love he always wanted from his father, Kevin felt more like a fan.

Trying to Win a Father's Approval

From an early age, Kevin saw how his dad's talents drew crowds. Because he was so proficient, people responded positively and liked him. Those experiences instilled in Kevin the belief that being good at something and drawing a crowd is the way to win attention and approval. Kevin says he realized only a few years ago that this approach wasn't working. "I used to believe that my main purpose in life was to gain the applause of the world," he says. "I needed people to approve of me. I wanted them to see me do something great, and I would not accept mediocrity."

For years Kevin believed that he had to be the best at whatever he did. If he got a role in a play, he had to be the lead. When he started boxing, he excelled. He even got into performing and producing music. Music became a passion for Kevin. His goal was to draw large crowds and win approval for his talent just like his dad had. He had an incessant need to prove himself. He went from one project to the next, and the process of seeking approval didn't stop.

"When I took on music, I took it to the next level. I started to do really well with my music, opening a studio and producing other people's work. Back then I was driven by a constant need for approval. If I didn't get the level of success I thought I was going to get, then I was on to the next thing, trying to reach it again."

But Kevin didn't become the best at things simply because he enjoyed them; he worked hard at them because he wanted to get his dad's attention. No matter what activity or sport it was, Kevin made up his mind that he was going to be the absolute best at it. Maybe one day his dad would finally give him the attention he craved. One day, during a time that his dad was in an alcohol rehab center, his father got a pass from rehab and came to watch Kevin's baseball game. Kevin remembers that day like it was yesterday. His dad showed up for him, and that made him feel both seen and loved.

As Kevin and I talk about his relationship with his dad, I want to know if there were any moments in which they did connect—moments when Kevin received the love that he wanted. "I do remember once when I was bowling, he said that he was excited that I was bowling well," Kevin says. "It was like fireworks were going off inside me. I was like, '*Oh my god, my dad is actually proud of me!*'" That memory brings a smile to Kevin's face, and his eyes brighten. But because such memories are so rare, Kevin immediately pivots to a memory of his dad that carries sadness.

Pride and Shame

Kevin took up boxing when he was young, and like most things he pursued, he became quite skilled. But naturally, when he first started, he wasn't very good. Every now and then, the gym in his hometown would set up matches between local boxers, and people in the community would come out to watch. One evening Kevin was scheduled to fight, but his opponent didn't show up. His coach told him, "The Canadian champ is here. His opponent is sick too, so we're going to do an exhibition between you two."

A rookie boxer fighting the Canadian champ? It sounded like a bad idea from the start, but Kevin agreed. Kevin's coach told him not to worry because the champ had agreed to go easy on him. It was just for show, to fill the space, so all he had to do was spar.

Kevin's voice softens as he tells the rest of the story. On that day, his dad and uncles came to see the fight. When Kevin saw them, he got nervous. He so badly wanted to please his dad, and this was an opportunity to make his father proud. Facing the champion boxer, Kevin recalls thinking, *I'm going to go up there and this guy is going to kill me.* So rather than simply sparring in an exhibition-type manner, Kevin says, he provoked a fight. "He knocked me out in like the second round," he says. "I went to throw a punch, and I remember my arm getting caught in the rope, and he just—boom—hits me." Kevin begins to tear up at the memory. "I'm sorry, this gets me," he says, wiping his eyes.

Getting knocked out in front of his dad made Kevin feel ashamed. Even though he was fighting someone far more experienced than he was, all Kevin could think about was the possibility of winning and making his dad proud. After all, the other guy was the champion boxer, and Kevin had had the courage to get in the ring with him.

When the Son Becomes the Parent

When Kevin and his brother needed their father at home, he was absent. Kevin's parents argued often, and eventually his mom left. That was a time when Kevin and his brother needed their dad most, but he was rarely home. "Things were falling apart, and my dad was nowhere to be found," Kevin remembers. "We couldn't find him unless we went to the bar. I remember feeling like I had to become the parent in our home."

This period was the most hurtful period in their relationship. His dad was gone every night, and Kevin and his brother would have to figure out dinner for themselves. Essentially, Kevin took over as head of household when he was only twelve years old. He picked up where his mom left off, including making his dad's lunches every morning. His dad treated things like nothing had changed. He'd just pick up his lunch from the fridge before heading to work and never thanked Kevin for making it for him. Kevin became a parent, just like that. It was never something he wanted to do, but he just took on the responsibility while feeling the pain of his father's absence even more.

Kevin still admired his father, and he could tell that his father admired him too. All of us have people we admire from a distance, but the love of a father is about connection. Like a fan, his dad admired him, but Kevin didn't want another fan; he wanted a father.

"Even to this day, I still feel like my dad admires the things I do, but what I really want is connection," he says. "In the past, he called me when his finances went bad. He calls me when he needs an oil change on his car. He calls me when he needs a loan. At times, I still feel like a parent to my dad."

"We play a lot of hockey in Canada, so I always wanted to play hockey as a kid," Kevin tells me. "I would go to the arena a lot and watch all my friends play hockey. They were always there with their dads. And so, I started to develop a relationship with my friends' dads because they would give me attention."

The other kids' parents would ask Kevin how he was doing and buy him something to eat. They made sure that he felt like part of the team, even though he wasn't. The way the other kids' parents treated him was what he always wanted from his dad.

Kevin got occasional glimpses of his father's pride in him. When Kevin was in his first band and started traveling around Canada and playing live concerts, he and the group had a good following of fans. For a while, his dad would come to every show and stand in the back.

"I remember thinking it was amazing that he came to every show," Kevin recounts. "One day I heard my dad bragging to one of his buddies about me at a local bar. I was kind of listening in, having a drink with my buddy, but I heard him say, 'Isn't that amazing that my son goes up there and does that? I don't know how he does it. It's amazing!'"

His dad rarely expressed his pride directly. Instead, Kevin had to overhear it.

Breaking the Cycle

Today their relationship is improving. With all the negative experiences Kevin shared from childhood, he expressed that God has shown him that hope is never dead and there is always the opportunity for change. "I guess you could say my dad is kind of like the prodigal father. Recently my dad and I were sitting at my house, and for some reason I got very emotional." Kevin told his dad how he felt as a child and how he interpreted his distance as lack of love. His father listened intently. When Kevin paused, his dad told him that he understood why his son would have felt a lack of love.

During that conversation, Kevin's father started to share some of his story with Kevin. Kevin listened and began to understand his dad better. His dad described losing his own father when he was just five years old, then having an abusive stepfather come into his life. "It didn't sound like an excuse; it sounded like a hurt child telling me how he never learned how to love properly," Kevin tells me now. "All of a sudden I felt enormous compassion for my father and for myself as well because I now knew we were both victims of a broken world and broken human love." For Kevin, it felt like in that moment of listening to his father and understanding him better, God was working to change their relationship and break the cycle.

Over the last couple of years, Kevin's dad has been making an effort to be a father to him. He visits for no other reason than just to hang out with his son. Every now and then he helps Kevin with his golf swing and randomly says the words that Kevin longed to hear as a child: "I'm proud of you."

"My dad is a good man, and now I can see that he is just an imperfect person trying to love as perfectly as he can," Kevin tells me now. "I'm in the same boat with my three children. I used to long for a hug from my father, or to hear the words *I love you*. Now after every visit my dad hugs me and tells me that he loves me—and he even says it first."

Being a Better Father

Kevin has been waiting for his dad to acknowledge him for most of his life. He's wanted to be seen and valued. As an adult working to heal and be a better father for his children, he hopes that his dad can begin a new path. A new chapter with his dad began with hearing him say he was sorry. "'I'm sorry for what you went through; I'm sorry for what we went through as a family'—that was amazing and healing for me," Kevin says. "I think it was also healing for him."

Kevin still hopes that his dad will continue to come over for no reason other than to hang out. "I still have this idea in my head of us just sitting on the couch, watching football or a Christmas movie together," he says. "It sounds silly, and it is nothing profound. It is just simple." His vision is one of peace and connection. Although Kevin says this imagined scenario isn't profound, it is. Unsolicited time and presence with a parent, without an agenda, is profound for those of us who never experienced it and have always wanted it.

Kevin and his wife, Jessica, have three children, ages eleven (Owen), nine (Kara), and five (Luke). Kevin tells me about each of his children, starting with the oldest and naming the ways he is trying to be the dad they need so that they will not inherit his story.

He's working to be more patient with Owen. He makes time to play games that Owen enjoys, and he listens to his stories about situations with friends without judging him or trying to fix things. "I always let him know that he does a good job," he says. "He is one of the good goal scorers on our hockey team, but he doesn't score all the time. Sometimes he doesn't do much at all, but I never hold him up to a standard. I just say, "Owen, man, you go out there and you play a great game. You didn't score. It doesn't matter. You did what you were supposed to do, and I'm proud of you. I don't need you to *be* the best, but I do want you to *try* your best."

Kevin's middle child, Kara, loves affection, so he spends time dancing with her. Like her dad, Kara has an ear for music. He finds time for the two of them to write music in the studio. They dance together and even come up with their own dance routines. Whenever she is worried or afraid, he finds ways to make her laugh that make the fear go away. For Kara, that's what love looks like. They also enjoy walking in nature. "She calls our times outside 'Daddy and Kara adventures.' It can be in the forest behind our house," he says with a smile. "Or sometimes she'll say, 'Dad, let's go for a star walk,' so we will just take off on a walk and I will teach her about the stars."

Unlike the others, Kevin's youngest child, Luke, has different boundaries when it comes to love. He doesn't care as much for physical affection as the others, but he enjoys time with his dad. Kevin is learning to honor who his son is, even at the age of five, and he is learning to love him the way that he needs. Luke loves to wrestle with his dad. When it comes to hugs, Luke likes to be the person who initiates, and Kevin welcomes it every time. "He likes to build stuff, and he is very hands-on," Kevin says. "Luke experiences love from me when I come into his world and play on his terms." When Kevin takes time to get down on the floor and play the way Luke wants to play, building stuff and following his rules, play becomes an act of love. He also gets to coach Luke in hockey.

Some might say his childhood memories have caused Kevin to "overcompensate" with displays of love, affection, and time. But I'm not so sure that as a parent you can ever overdo it when it comes to those three things!

When Love Jumps into Your Arms

A few years ago, Kevin started looking inward and asking himself hard questions: *Why am I doing these things? What am I doing here? What am I trying to prove?* "That was the beginning of a process to realize that I am enough," Kevin says. "I am worthy of love, and I don't have to prove anything."

Things are different for Kevin now. He still writes, sings, and produces, but he does it because he loves it instead of for approval.

From time to time, he still has to resist the urge to do things solely for the purpose of getting his dad's approval. To stop himself, Kevin has come up with some centering questions that he can ask himself. When he realizes that he's about to do something because he is longing for his dad's approval, he stops and asks himself: *Why am I doing this? Is this something I'm passionate about? Does it bring me joy? Or am I doing it to try to garner someone's attention, approval, or love?* After sitting with the questions and finding his way toward answers, Kevin has gotten better at making healthy choices.

As a father, Kevin gives his children the love that they need, and the wounded child within him is finally getting the love he's always deserved. Kevin no longer has to be afraid. He and his wife have created the peaceful, happy home that he missed out on as a child.

Sometimes the love and attention that we have been waiting for doesn't come from the person we needed it from. But we are rewarded when we open ourselves up to receive that love, however it chooses to show up. At one point in his life, when Kevin desired attention from his father, he'd take it from anyone willing to offer it. Now he's getting it from his children. He's getting it from people who deeply love him. Attention and love are no longer things he has to go looking for; he doesn't have to chase them. They're at home. Every day when he walks in the door after a long day at work, love comes running and jumps into his arms.

Takeaways

Kevin's "I Wish My Dad" story shows the burden of being raised by a parent who was absent more than present. Narcissism is a personality disorder that includes an inflated sense of self-importance, the need for an extensive supply of attention and admiration, and a lack of empathy for others. Someone who tends toward narcissism has a hyper-confidence that often shrouds a frail self-esteem. Children of narcissistic parents, like Kevin, sometimes overhear this parent bragging about them to others but rarely experience the validation or emotional support directly. Narcissistic parents often need the conversation to be about them; they exhibit immature and selfish behavior, and can make people feel bad for not doing what they want immediately.

Kevin's childhood was further challenged by becoming a "parentified" child: a child forced to take on adult responsibilities. Parentification is very traumatizing. Kevin not only became a parent figure to his older brother but also to his own father. He continues to carry this pattern into his adulthood as he meets his dad's needs while simultaneously meeting the needs of his own household. Adult sons whose fathers are still living often look for what they need from their fathers, and sometimes they need to learn to set boundaries with their fathers.

The joy in Kevin's story is that, through parenting his own children, he can now give his inner child what he longed to receive from his father. Every time he acknowledges Owen's willingness to play hockey whether he wins or loses, takes a star walk with Kara, or gets down on the floor and builds things with Luke—every time he does these things, he disrupts the generational pattern of absent fathers. Because of his determination to be the change he desires to see in his father, he becomes the father to Owen, Kara, and Luke that he did not have.

Just as unhealthy patterns can be passed down from generation to generation, so can healthy patterns. Men who have children can heal themselves and future generations by rewriting the stories bequeathed to them. Even though their own fathers lacked the capacity to give them what they needed, they can write new, life-giving chapters for their children.

CHAPTER 9

I WISH MY DAD DIDN'T ABANDON ME

VANCE

Vance is the epitome of a gentle giant. I don't know exactly how tall he is, but I can tell you this: I'm six foot two, and he hovers over me.

Vance is an affectionate person. He could be called a hugger for sure, and he exudes a positive, energetic, and warm personality. When talking to him, you know that you are seen and valued. People love Vance, and those who know him will do just about anything for him. He's respected as a person and as a leader. Listening to Vance's "I Wish My Dad" story gave me a lens into how he became the hugging and loving gentle giant that he is today.

As Vance was growing up, his dad was not around. Everything he knows about him is based on what he has heard from family members, friends, and women who were in his dad's life. Like so many of the men I interviewed, Vance was shaped by his father's absence as much as many boys are shaped by their fathers' presence. Although his father wasn't around much, one painful statement Vance's dad made to his mom remains with him all these years later. "My mom and dad were arguing, and she asked him, 'How is it possible for you to treat me so badly and still say you care?'"

Vance looks me straight in the eye as he tells me his father's answer. "He said, 'Never overestimate your value to anyone.'"

This message—don't assume people love you even if they say they do—stuck with Vance, and not only as a comment directed at his mother. Vance understood that cruel sentence applied to him as well. Because when Vance's dad told his mom that she shouldn't overestimate her value, Vance realized that he couldn't assume anything about how much his dad valued *him*. "I mean, if he didn't value my mom, then how could he possibly value me?"

Know Who You Are and Where You Came From

Now in his sixties, Vance is a Methodist pastor. He is married to Bridgett and has three adult children from a previous marriage. Vance's father died when he was thirty-seven years old. His dad was sixty-four. "If I combined the number of days I spent with him over the span of thirty-seven years, it wouldn't add up to a month," he tells me. "So I have very few personal memories of life with him." His father was the youngest of four boys and, from what others have told him, his dad was a very thoughtful man. He was an intellectual, having studied sociology at Temple University. He finished all the coursework for his PhD but didn't finish writing his dissertation. He was a lecturer at one university and an assistant professor for a time at another.

Of the limited memories Vance has of time he spent with his dad, the fondest memory he has is from when he was thirteen years old. He and his brother went to a bookstore with their dad, and he bought Vance two books: *The Souls of Black Folk* by W. E. B. Du Bois and *To Be a Slave* by Julius Lester. He kept those books for a long time, and that day was so important to Vance that on each of his three children's thirteenth birthdays, he gave them copies of *To Be a Slave*.

It is apropos that the fondest memory Vance has of his father includes these two books, which are important texts in the African American canon. They offer the meaning of identity for Black people living on American soil. Du Bois offers the idea of "double consciousness" as a lens through which to understand the way that Black people look at themselves through the eyes of whiteness. "It is a peculiar sensation, this double-consciousness, this sense of always looking at one's self through the eyes of others, of measuring one's soul by the tape of a world that looks on in amused contempt and pity," Du Bois writes toward the beginning of the book. "One feels his two-ness—an American, a Negro; two souls, two thoughts, two unreconciled strivings; two warring ideals in one dark body, whose dogged strength alone keeps it from being torn asunder."

The other book, *To Be a Slave*, offers personal accounts told by formerly enslaved people. In buying these books for his son, Vance's father offered some implicit messages: know who you are, and know where you come from. Vance's father had a brilliant mind, and he could likely theorize about how Black people's identities were shaped by the history of chattel slavery and Jim Crow. Yet he apparently lacked the capacity to analyze how his own absence and hurtful words would shape his son's identity.

Vance grew up during the Civil Rights era. He came to respect the nonviolent views of Rev. Dr. Martin Luther King Jr. taught to him by his mother and grandmother. Vance chose to follow their nonviolent teaching on his path in life and as way to deal with conflict. "Being a Black boy raised by two women during the days of Martin Luther King and choosing nonviolence—well, I had to deal with people whipping my ass all the time," he says. Colorism—prejudice against people with darker skin—is an issue in many Black communities, and it's rarely discussed in public spaces. It's often argued that African Americans of darker complexion experience more discrimination across the board and are the victims of more violence than those of lighter hues.

"I am the darkest person in the family and felt that my father could have helped me deal with the challenges I had to face," Vance says. "As a kid I thought people didn't like me because I'm dark. I was young, so I didn't have the wisdom to know that my skin tone wasn't the issue—it was their racism."

Vance believes his dad could have guided him through learning to be proud of who he was becoming as Black man. Love would have looked like having a father who was present to protect and guide him through the challenges of growing up as a Black male in America. Buying his son books was a wonderful gesture, but it's unfortunate that his guidance on these matters started and stopped with that act.

Because Vance has been dealing with his story for a while now, it is easy for him to share it with me. As he talks to me, he seems to detach any emotion from the story. It's often easier for us to think and talk about difficult things related to our fathers when we don't let ourselves feel them. "I have real abandonment issues," he tells me matter-of-factly. "My mother and father took me to my grandmother's house in Bluefield, West Virginia, while they moved to Trenton, New Jersey. My mother came back, but my dad never did. I was one year old. Five years later, my mom got pregnant by my dad again, with my brother Vince, and then my dad left again. Vince was sent to be raised by my aunt in New York. Two years later, my grandparents separated and then divorced. Three years later, my mother, my two brothers, and my sister all left and moved to New York, and I was left with my grandmother. So by the time I was ten years old, about ten people had left my life."

He pauses, leans forward, and then lays it on the line: "So when I hear, 'Never overestimate your value to anyone,' that becomes a core feeling for me. Because no one stayed."

Afraid to Be Like the Man He Didn't Know

Love was always present for Vance, however, through his grand-mother. She is evidence that if we broaden our lens to look beyond what hurts, sometimes we see that love has always been present.

One day when Vance was young, his grandmother sent him to the store. On his way, a neighbor, Mr. Austin, yelled for Vance to come over. He wanted to tell Vance a story about his dad. Mr. Austin was in Korea with Vance's father during the Korean War. He told Vance that one day they were sitting in a bar, drinking, when a guy walked up to Vance's dad and accused him of steal-ing something from him. Vance's dad told the guy that he didn't know what he was talking about. The man persisted and then threatened Vance's dad. At that point Vance's dad put down his drink and knocked the guy out. Then he calmly finished his drink, paid the bartender, and left the bar.

"I was always learning things about him from other people and trying to put the pieces together in an effort to know him in some distant way," Vance says. Several years ago, a woman named Judy called Vance out of the blue, introduced herself, and said that she wanted to tell him some things about his dad. She and his dad had a relationship for several years, and she wanted to help Vance understand the issues his dad wrestled with a little better. His dad was a communications specialist on the front lines, which is where most Black men were positioned in Korea. Judy shared that Vance's dad was addicted to heroin when he left the service. She said that he saw so many traumatic things happen in Korea, but he never wanted to talk about it. He was aloof and emotionally distant at times. "So I can't know for sure, but I'm thinking his previous addiction to heroin contrib-uted to his distance and what seemed like a lack of empathy," Vance reflects. "He couldn't bear pain after seeing so much. He lived with trauma coming out of the war, and he dealt with it by self-medicating."

These stories allowed Vance to see that the question of why his father wasn't around had no easy answers. He was a complicated man. The stories didn't make his absence any easier to live with, but they did help Vance put together some pieces.

Vance's dad died at the age of sixty-four. At the time that I interview Vance, he is in his early sixties and dealing with some health concerns himself. Knowing how old his dad was when he died has triggered fears in Vance, and he has developed an anxiety around the fear of death. "Over the years, people tell me how much I look like him, sound like him, walk like him," he says. "At some points I almost tried to stay away from people who knew him because I didn't want to hear it. I was scared to be like him."

Vance admired his dad's passion for learning and teaching, but he is afraid of inheriting the negative characteristics. For Vance, being like his father would look like not taking care of his health, not caring for his kids, and being dependent on drugs. His dad had an addiction problem, and while he eventually overcame it, he remained distant and aloof. Vance has frequently been afraid of becoming the same kind of person.

"I didn't want to be the kind of person who said hurtful things to the people they love, and I didn't want to be the kind of father who wasn't present for my children. So I have been very mindful to be a good person who is reliable and available to the people who love me and rely on my presence. In that way I am not like my dad. I'm reliable."

Vance has been determined not to be the kind of man who would make people feel unloved. Sometimes we learn who we want to be by seeing who our parents weren't.

Finding the Missing Pieces

Vance has lived with a lot of questions that he wishes his dad could have answered. He wanted to fill in blanks that he's lived with for so long. Vance still wants to know: *Did his dad regret things he did that were not acts of love? Were there other people his dad hurt emotionally, and what did he wish he could have offered to them?* For Vance, those questions are really about wanting to know if his dad regretted not being present for his children, and if he regretted the emotional pain it causes them to this day. He still doubts that his dad ever loved him. "I don't believe he came anywhere close to loving me," he says. "Another thing I haven't thought about in years that he said to my mother was: 'You can't love anyone you don't know.' Those are his words."

We sit together in silence for a moment. "I mean, he never really knew me. If that's what he believed, then how could he love me?"

But Vance's desire to know more about his dad is complicated too. Sometimes he wants to know more about his dad, and other times he has wanted to disassociate himself from anything having to do with him. "I wanted to distance myself from him because, from everything I can tell, I was the first problem he had. I'm the eldest of his children, and I feel like I'm the one he didn't want."

Vance explains to me that his grandmother had high aspirations for her daughter, Vance's mom, that she did not pursue because she got pregnant with Vance. Vance's dad was on a football scholarship in college. The coach found out about the pregnancy and told Vance's dad that if he did not marry her, he would lose his scholarship. They got married eight days before Vance was born. "Knowing this story, I have always believed that my father resented my presence because he was forced to get married in order to keep his scholarship."

Vance's dad never referred to him as a burden. Nor did he ever tell Vance that he resented his birth. Given the changes his dad had to make to his life once Vance's mom was pregnant, Vance assumed that he was a burden for his father.

The pain that Vance carries because of these thoughts is often hard for him to put in words. Feeling like he was born a burden has manifested into self-doubt over the years, but

Vance has pushed through it. He treats people well, works to address the needs of vulnerable poor communities, and is highly respected by peers across the country. "God has been able to elevate me despite my self-doubt and life-limiting beliefs of not feeling worthy," he says. "I admit that I have doubts and know they're connected to how I feel about myself because of my dad, but I keep moving forward, trusting God to make a way."

I am kind of shocked when Vance refers to himself as being his dad's burden. I want to know more. Vance goes on to lay out a full picture that, for him, justifies his feelings. It may very well be how he feels, but feeling something doesn't make it true at all. As my therapist once told me: "Your feelings serve your thoughts, and your thoughts serve you. Change your thoughts, and how you feel will change too."

Vance knows that feelings don't always tell us the truth. Feeling that you're a burden to someone doesn't mean you are. "In therapy, I'm working to see this issue as being about who *he* was and not about *me*," he says. "For more than fifty years, I have been blaming myself. It has been helpful to get clarity. Therapy is helping me do better with realizing that it was his choice to not be there for me as a father. I didn't make any choices."

Now in his sixties, Vance is still working to heal the story that he's been telling himself about his own value and learning to trust that everyone who loves him will not leave him. He's learning to accept that he is worthy of love—and always has been.

Vance continues to wrestle with this question as he seeks to heal the story he's been telling himself about his value. In therapy, Vance is learning to see that his value is not defined by the person his dad was not.

Being an Affectionate Father

Vance is very self-aware when it comes to what he needs emotionally from the people in his life in order to feel loved. This self-awareness is connected to the trauma of not having his father around when he was a child. His son Bryant, who is in his thirties now, still hugs and kisses his dad like he did when he was a little boy. When all of his children were young, Vance was intentional about making sure they heard from him if he was traveling or not able to be physically present. Remembering how not hearing from his own father caused him to question if he was loved? That was something he never wanted his children to experience.

He gives them lots of hugs too—and when they were young, he made sure to pick them up. "I've always been big, even when I was a young guy," he says. "I was bigger than all the other kids. Adults would not lift me up because I was too big. They would pick up my brothers and my sister, but no one picked me up. I decided at a young age that if I ever had children, I was going to pick them up and hug them because I know what it feels like not to be picked up."

Vance continues to see a therapist for help with overcoming the self-doubt created by his childhood story. He is learning to disconnect who he is now from the man his father was not. He's learning to offer himself the love that he's always wanted to experience and realize that he's always deserved it. He's not responsible for what his parents were incapable of doing when he was a child. How he loves others and allows himself to be loved breaks the cycle for his children, grandchildren, and future generations.

Vance's dad's words to his mom so many years ago—about not overestimating her value—have stuck with him to this day. He doesn't have a problem offering love to others, but he still wrestles with letting love in.

Takeaways

Vance's "I Wish My Dad" story is filled with grappling with the double consciousness that Du Bois describes so well. Being a statuesque Black man growing up during the Civil Rights era, being abandoned by his father, navigating complicated grief, and watching the exodus of so many loved ones from his life by the age of ten: Vance's ability to create his own life in light of all that is a miracle.

The vibration of his father's words—*Never overestimate your value to anyone*—lives in Vance's body and has become an internalized core value. These and other painful messages—married with the absence of his father, grief, and the violence Vance faced because of his dark hue and his choice to be nonviolent—can culminate into complex trauma.

Vance's father was the survivor of traumatizing events as well. We can only imagine what he experienced serving in the army on the front lines during the Korean War. He then arrived home, became a father and husband, and went through college, still carrying the trauma of war in his body. He tried to escape the visceral nature of trauma through his heroin addiction, and that addiction pushed him further away from himself and his sons.

How does a father muster up a presence and love for others when he doesn't have the capacity to do it for himself? How can a father show up for his sons when he cannot show up for himself? It is clear that Vance's father wrestled with his own layered identities and passed this down to his sons.

Vance's faith, kindness, and commitment to his own healing in therapy will help him untether himself from his father's pathologies. Vance has taken responsibility to break a generational cycle of absence and abandonment through being a dedicated and active father in the lives of his three children. Through parenting his children, he has the opportunity to parent himself in the ways he longed for.

CHAPTER 10

I WISH MY DAD KEPT HIS PROMISES

ANDRE

A few years ago, I was looking for a contractor to do some work in my kitchen. A colleague highly recommended Andre, who turned out to be one of kindest people I've ever met. He has such a positive, gentle, and caring spirit. As a contractor, he takes pride in doing a great job and going the extra mile to exceed expectations. He also genuinely cares about people. He doesn't just care about his work; he cares about you.

Becoming a contractor and helping people improve their homes is a second act for Andre. Having retired from playing professional football, he decided to pursue his dream of owning a home improvements company. He pursues his dreams and has a knack for making them happen.

Like several other men I talked to, Andre's own experience with his father differed from the way he heard other people talk about his father. That disconnect—the way sons experience their fathers and the way other people describe them—was a theme of many of the "I Wish My Dad" stories I heard.

Andre's dad was an absentee father, whom he saw mostly on holidays. But he admired that so many people respected his dad, and he always wished they had more time together. From childhood into his adult years, Andre grew accustomed to his father breaking his promises. "He always made empty promises," Andre reflects. "He would say he was going to do something, but he would never follow up."

The persistent question during his childhood became: *Would his father show up—or not?*

Getting to Know Dad in Spurts

Andre's dad was very well known in his hometown of Akron, Ohio, where he worked for the city. Tall, handsome, and charismatic, he was the type of guy who didn't have an enemy.

Andre saw his dad when he came around for big holidays, like the Fourth of July or Easter. He would pick up Andre and his brother Darryl for cookouts hosted by his side of the family. They were being raised by their mom and grandmother, so holidays with Dad were a time to meet aunts, uncles, and cousins on the other side of the family. Even though he was absent most of the time, Andre always looked up to him with admiration and respect because people who knew his dad held him in high regard. He was a bigger-than-life kind of personality—the life of the party. When Andre went to family reunions with him, everyone hovered around him.

Only seeing his dad during holidays, though, didn't create a lot of opportunities for Andre to cultivate the kind of close relationship he wanted. "My familiarity with my dad was always in spurts—there, gone, there, gone," he tells me. "One song by the Temptations probably fits him well: 'Papa was a rolling stone, wherever he laid his hat was his home.'"

On the rare occasions when Andre did get time with his dad, he was attentive and caring. As a kid, Andre recalls, he was always trying to impress his dad with the hope of hearing him say that he was proud. Andre got involved in sports at a very young age. He played just about every sport—track, basketball, football, and baseball—and was very good at all of them.

His mom worked long hours as the only provider for him and his brother. She didn't drive, so she took public transportation to and from work—a commute that made her days even longer. Most of his childhood, he had to be responsible for getting himself to and from practice. His dad's inability to be present for small things, like rides to and from practice, became significant sad memories. "I was the kid who had to ride with someone else's parents," he says.

Growing up without his dad, Andre knew that he was missing something. He didn't have a father showing him how to navigate life. Andre saw how other kids were able to learn from their fathers and pick up new skills or hobbies. "I saw other kids with their dads," he says. "If Dad was a mechanic, he taught his son how to be a mechanic. Or if Dad was an accountant, the son followed in his footsteps." It wasn't that Andre wanted to follow in his father's specific footsteps, but he longed for the opportunity to glean life lessons and learn new skills. It was about having a dad who invested time. Andre says it would have been nice to have grown up with a father who modeled responsibility for him instead of having to learn it on his own. "I was just wanting to be a better man, but not knowing really what that looked like because he wasn't there to show me."

Despite his father's absence, Andre achieved the things he wanted for himself. He wanted his dad to be there for him during important moments. He wanted his dad to teach him life lessons and skills. But he learned those life lessons from other people in his life. "Even though my dad didn't show me love, other males in my life—like my high school sweetheart's dad, my wife's dad, my godfather—showed me the love I was yearning for. Even my godfather, Jim, stepped in when my dad wasn't there."

Andre discovered his love for home improvements while he was a professional athlete. He had always wanted to buy his grandmother a new home, but he knew that she was never going to leave the house she owned. "I knew she wasn't leaving, so the next best thing was to make her house better. When I got my signing bonus from the Cincinnati Bengals, I took that money to help renovate my grandmother's house. It was my dream and passion as a kid to one day be able to do something for her."

After fulfilling his childhood dream for his grandmother, Andre dreamed of doing home improvements. When he retired from professional football, he started his own business and loves it. Only later did Andre learn that his grandfather had been a master carpenter. "I can't say that those skill sets were passed down to me," he says. "I kind of fell into them—only to find out through my uncle that the thing I love was the thing my grandfather loved too." He pauses to reflect. "It is just something missing in a person's life when half of their identity is absent."

Will He Show Up?

Andre is very humble, so sometimes during our conversation I have to pull information out of him about his college and NFL football career. He tells me that every now and then, up until he went to college, his dad would show up at sporting events. Those moments meant so much to Andre that he remembers every single game at which he saw his dad in the stands. He came to a game when Andre was in the sixth grade and a couple of high school games. But Andre's father didn't attend any of his college football games. He didn't come to any of his NFL games. "As a matter of fact, he didn't set foot on Bowling Green State University's campus until I was inducted into their Hall of Fame," he says.

Andre simply got used to expecting the worst from his dad when it came to showing up for him. As Andre was preparing to be inducted into the Football Hall of Fame at Bowling Green, he told his dad about the induction ceremony and invited him to attend. His dad told Andre that he would love to be there. "At one point I was hesitant to even tell him," Andre says now. "But I did, and I even followed up as the ceremony date was approaching." His father reiterated his promise that he would be there.

I can imagine a younger Andre in my mind as he tells this story, waiting and wondering as the day approached if his father would come through. Remember: his dad never showed up for a game during his college and professional football years. Would that day be any different?

On the day of the induction ceremony Andre was anxious, and he decided to call his father while en route to the venue. "I called him, and it sounded like he had forgotten," he tells me. "That took me back to my childhood disappointments. I said, 'The ceremony is going to be this evening. I hope you can make it.'"

Lo and behold, Andre's father did show up. "That felt good," he recounts simply. "It took my acceptance speech in a totally different direction, one that brought me to tears. I was up there giving my speech and connecting with him at that moment."

Andre was forty-four when he was inducted into the Hall of Fame. His dad had never seen him play a college or professional game. He was there, though, for a capstone moment of Andre's career. It didn't take away the legacy of broken promises and absence, but it did prove to be a healing moment and monumental day for Andre, his dad, and their father–son relationship.

Taking the Risk to Reach Out

Andre was fifty years old before he spent the night at his father's house. Andre was in Akron for an unrelated family matter concerning his mom. It just so happened that it was also Father's Day weekend. Andre knew where his dad lived, and he figured he might as well try to see his dad. When he arrived, he asked his dad if they could go out for a drink. Andre isn't much of a drinker, but he knew his dad was, so Andre's invitation was about getting some time with his father on his father's terms. During their conversation, Andre learned that his dad had started going to church. Andre's Christian faith is an essential part of his life, so he was excited by that news. They were able to go to church together the next day. These were the types of experiences Andre had always longed for.

Andre wanted to maximize the time he had with his father when they went out for a drink that Saturday evening, so he jumped right in. He took the risk of being vulnerable with his father by sharing feelings that he'd been holding in for years. "I said, 'Dad, you really didn't support me the way I would have loved for you to. I was a model student and got a scholarship playing college ball. I played professional football, and you really weren't a part of any of that.'"

During their conversation at the bar, he told his dad that he had never heard him say that he loved him. His father listened carefully as Andre shared his heart and then responded. "My dad's response was, 'Son, I thought you knew.' He broke down and said, 'I love you. And I am proud of your accomplishments and the man you turned out to be.'"

I wonder if his father's tears were filled with the regret of missed opportunities to express his love and pride for Andre. Andre finally got to hear the words he had been waiting for his entire life. From that point on, it was easier for him and his dad to say "I love you" to each other—although it still was not easy.

Finishing Well with Dad

Andre's stepmother had always sent Andre cards for birthdays and Christmas to maintain the family connection. So when his dad was in the hospital and it was clear that he was dying, Andre appreciated that she was the person who reached out to Andre. "She said, 'I know you guys didn't really spend a lot of time together, but here is an opportunity for you to say good-bye if you want to.' She said she'd understand if I didn't want to come."

After hearing from his stepmom, Andre reached out to his older brother and told him the news. He told his brother that he thought they needed to grapple with a few questions. How they responded in this moment would define their stories, not their dad's. "When I was on the phone with my brother, I said, 'What do we want to do? Do we want to be remembered as his kids that didn't show up? Or do we want to be bigger than that and show up for him?'"

Given the kind of man Andre is, the answers were clear. He picked up his brother and they drove to Akron to be with their dad at the hospital. Andre was at his dad's bedside when he took his last breath. "In the end, I forgave him for not being there for me. I prayed with him to receive Christ in that moment because I want to see him again. My belief is that once we pass from this earth, those who commit their lives to Christ will see their loved ones again. I guess I am holding on to the fact that we didn't have the best relationship here on earth, but maybe we will be able to reconnect and have a relationship in heaven."

His dad's funeral was standing room only. "People lined up outside the door," Andre says. "I would hear stories from some of those people once they found out I was Andre. They said, 'Your father would always talk about you playing football.'"

Those comments brought conflicting emotions. It was good to know that his dad had spoken highly of him to other people. Yet those were words he always wanted to hear straight from his dad, not from guests at his funeral. Andre is grateful for their conversation over drinks several years prior, and although they couldn't make up for a lifetime of broken promises and missed opportunities, they do provide some comfort.

Holding onto Messages from Dad

Andre's eyes light up when he tells me one last memory of his father. It's in the form of a voicemail from his dad that he has kept it on his phone for more than a decade now.

Before his father died, Andre had taken down the gutters of his mom's house and was going to throw them away. But he remembered that his dad always found ways to make extra money and that selling scrap metal was one of them. "So I left him a message saying, 'Hey, Dad, if you want these gutters, they're over here and you can have them.'"

His father called back and left a voicemail. Now, in my office, Andre pulls out his phone and plays the message for me. "Hey, man, thanks for those awnings off the house. I'm glad you called me. I can use them. They took care of business for me. I just called to tell you thank you. Have a good day."

The message is brief, about seventeen seconds long. It's so simple. So normal. But in that moment, as we listen to his dad's voice, Andre begins to cry. "The message reminds me of how much I miss him," he says through his tears. "How little time we did spend together."

These days, being mindful of what he missed out on with his dad, Andre makes every effort to do things differently so that his children will have the memories he doesn't. He wants his children to have more than a voicemail to confirm his love and care for them. And he has decided this: the next best thing to having a dad who kept his promises is becoming a dad who keeps his.

Andre and his wife, Randi, have three adult children: Allison, Michael, and Justin. Andre is building a new legacy of what fatherhood looks like for his family and doing his best to teach his kids how to do it should they ever get their turn. One of the biggest lessons he wants them to know is that true love often requires forgiveness. "I have love for my dad despite his absence," Andre says. "I still yearn to be with him, to love him, and to be loved by him. I still wish I could capture that, but I know he's gone. I don't hold a grudge or anger against him because I had a choice. Either I could be like my dad or try to be the dad that someone would be proud to have."

Listening to Andre, I can say with confidence that he has chosen the latter.

Takeaways

Andre's "I Wish My Dad" story captures the impact a father's absence has on a son—a son who prioritizes gaining the attention of his father. This type of attention-seeking behavior is constructive and often overlooked by parents, particularly those who are absent. Andre's father undervalued his own presence and voice in Andre's life. He made the assumption that Andre already knew he was proud of him. But the active voice of a father in a son's life matters. How can someone know how you feel about them if you never articulate it?

Many fathers, like Andre's, carry a lot of insecurities and even surmise that their children are better off without them. The shadow parts of fathers may cause them to distance themselves from those who love them the most—their children. This becomes a cycle: the shame they carry about their absence accrues, and they distance themselves even more.

Why was Andre's father unable to tell the truth about not being present? Broken promises cause harm and leave sons with miscarried expectations and constant disappointment. Sons internalize a father's absence as a signal that they themselves are not good enough or worthy enough—even if a father's absence has nothing to do with them.

Sometimes parents measure themselves against their children and feel unworthy of being present in their lives. A father's journey with shame, insecurity, and unworthiness, when left unhealed, is often manifested in their children. Fathers, remember that your sons are not your competition or your measuring stick. They are your admirers who desire to have you close.

Andre was blessed to have other men serve as positive role models and father figures. Andre models intentionality about healing and a son's journey to a place of acceptance. Andre eventually accepted that his father showed love as he was able. Andre became responsible for healing his childhood wounds by initiating conversations with his father, in which he expressed the impact of his father's absence to him directly. Andre continues to heal himself by choosing to maintain an active presence in the lives of his own children each day.

CHAPTER 11

I WISH MY DAD WAS LOYAL TO OUR HOME

RUDY

Rudy is the most generous person I know. He always sees the potential in people, no matter how bad their mistakes or how many times they mess up. He's the embodiment of forgiveness and generosity. His life is guided by a six-word sentence: *He loved like it mattered most.* He and his wife, Juanita, are the best example of a marriage of teamwork that I've ever seen. They are authors, humanitarians, and co-pastors of a church in Houston, Texas, as well as co-founders of an organization that provides services to the unhoused of Houston. They have two children: Morgan, thirty-four, and Ryan, thirty-three. Rudy and Juanita will tell you that marriage is not always easy and getting to where they are was no cakewalk. But they've managed to do it by loving each other for who they are and not expecting each other to become someone they're not. Their friendship and love are admirable and inspiring.

Rudy's journey with his dad is complicated, to say the least. They were business partners and friends. Every so often he shares a story about his dad that gives me a lens into a complicated man with a laser focus on what mattered most to him: making business deals.

Rudy's dad had rules and values he expected others to follow, and rules he was willing to break if doing so benefited him. Loyalty was important to his dad, but loyalty also had fluid boundaries. When it came to his best friends, he was loyal to a fault. When it came to marriage, loyalty became more fluid, and apparently, in his father's mind, didn't require honesty or fidelity.

Periodically, Rudy's father would ask Rudy if he wanted to go for a ride with him. He loved hanging out with his dad, so the answer was always yes. But going out with his dad complicated things for Rudy at home. Going out with his dad came with learning to keep secrets.

Born to Hustle

Rudy's dad was the youngest of fourteen siblings and was raised by his older sister from the age of eleven. He was very close to his siblings and even owned several businesses with his sister. The family was very industrious. Even though he was the youngest, Rudy's dad was the brother his siblings could count on. "He was like the hero of the family," Rudy tells me. "He was smart. He went to college, got a master's degree in accounting. But he was also a hustler. And he was a hustler because his older brothers were hustlers. They had multiple businesses and ways to make money. Some were legal and some were not."

Rudy's dad carried trauma from his own childhood. "Looking back on it, I realize he was abandoned by his mother and his father," Rudy says. Rudy's dad had no real connection with his parents. His older sister and her husband cared for him. His sister's husband had other women and disrespected his wife. That's what Rudy's dad saw modeled, and it shaped who he was becoming. His brother-in-law was his father figure.

Rudy says that his dad also lived under the weight of a lot of fear. Two of his brothers were murdered, and because of that, Rudy says, his father was always preparing him for his untimely death. "He never expected to make it, never expected to live, he always expected someone was going to kill him. All of that amounted to pressure. My mom and I were the recipients of that fear and pressure."

On the one hand, Rudy's dad was gregarious and principled. "If he told you he was going to do something, he was going to do it," Rudy recalls. "If he told you he was going to get you, he was going to get you. Whatever he told you he was going to do—well, you could put money on that." He took friendship seriously. People he considered friends could count on him.

Yet as Rudy grew up, his father's business was running what Rudy has called a "borderline brothel"—borderline in the sense that the women were independent contractors. He and his father owned the motel during the time that crack was hitting the streets. "Our rooms ultimately became places where more crack was smoked than sex was sold," Rudy has said in an interview.

At times, his loyalty to friends took precedence over his loyalty to Rudy's mom. "It was always a struggle for him and my mom. There was always an argument after my dad would do something for one of his friends. He didn't have a lot of people he considered friends. My entire childhood, there were only five men who ever came to our house. He was committed to them— sometimes to the detriment of keeping peace in our home."

Rudy's dad knew everyone in the streets, but there were only four guys he really considered his best friends: Johnny, John, Alonzo, and William. Whatever they were going through, Rudy's dad supported them, and they did the same for him. "So if they needed money, he would put up the money. If they were going through some shit, he would go through the shit with them. Their problems became his problem to help them solve."

Even though his dad's friendships were a point of relationship tension between his parents, Rudy still thinks of them as good friends for his dad and admires their friendships. "I still befriend with the same values and standards for friendship I learned from my dad," Rudy reflects.

His father's shadow side was his love for being in the streets. "I always felt he was better in the streets than he was at home," Rudy says. People in the streets thought Rudy's dad was a wonderful guy: charismatic, fun, and friendly. "I would periodically get a glimpse of that warm and kind person who people outside of our home knew him to be," Rudy tells me. "Whenever he was leaving the house to be in the streets, I would always hop in the car, because I would get to experience the kind person everyone else knew."

But at home Rudy knew him as a hard, distant authoritarian. He had high expectations for Rudy, who felt the pressure to excel academically. Rudy was extremely smart and did well in school but struggled in math. His dad was brilliant at math and couldn't understand why his son was having problems grasping it. Rudy would experience his dad's dark side during their evening homework ritual. "During those moments he would get so frustrated and mean," Rudy recalls. "I couldn't help but ask myself in frustration: *Where is the guy who everyone loves out there?* That guy was left at the door, but my mom and I got the dark side. I wanted him to show me the same kindness that he showed people outside our home. Even when I made mistakes— especially when I made mistakes."

Rudy experienced a harsh authoritarian. His mom experienced a serial adulterer.

Keeping Dad's Secrets

Some of Rudy's father's daily activities would be considered those of a good husband and family man. He would come home every evening, for instance, and would sit down and eat dinner with Rudy and his wife. "No matter what he had going on in the streets he would stop, come home, and sit down to eat," Rudy says. On the surface, that might look and sound like a man committed to family relationships. But the events that followed signaled something else. "After he finished eating, after he worked with me on the homework, he would go back to the streets, every day."

His dad's commitment to always coming home for dinner reminds me of an image Ta-Nehisi Coates paints of his dad in his memoir *The Beautiful Struggle*. "There were days I would have wished him into nothing, so that I could be free to relish in dumb shit with all the other laughing, orphaned boys," Coates writes. "There were others, when I looked around and saw that, though the birthright of every child was a manned fortress, we lived in unnatural times. All the guardians had fled their posts, and here was mine, his hand on his sword, his armor glimmering in the light of moons."

Rudy's dad was a complicated man, to say the least. But I can still see the value and impact of what it meant for him to always come home for dinner. In a sense, he never surrendered his post, in spite of all his faults. In his own peculiar way, he remained a guardian of his post, of the 'manned fortress' that was his home."

Rudy wasn't even six years old when he first started going for rides with his dad. Riding with his dad and hanging out in the streets meant they were going to make some stops that typically included his dad visiting women. "I remember sitting in the car one day when my dad stopped by this house to see one particular lady that my mom accused him of having an affair with," Rudy reflects. "My mom knew a little bit more about this one than she did about any of the other women. The lady in that house looked at me through the screen door, and I felt very uneasy with the way she was looking at me."

Rudy stops the story and then starts in again, talking about that day like it had just happened. Sometimes childhood memories stand out so clearly like that—like they were yesterday. "So I get back home with my dad, and I have to lie to my mom. My mom says, 'Where were you?' I say, 'I was X, Y, Z.'"

Having to lie to one parent to protect the other is beyond confusing for a child. "So I wasn't just riding with my dad," Rudy says. "I was his alibi. It was very uncomfortable."

Rudy decided very early in his life what kind of husband he wanted to be. He didn't like the accusations, lying, and secrets. Keeping things from his mom about his dad's behavior in the streets was painful, and Rudy didn't want that for himself. "Because of what I experienced with my dad, I was only about ten years old when I made a fidelity commitment as a result of those runs," he says. "I would tell myself, *If I ever get married, I'm not going to cheat on my wife.*"

Dad Was a Present Provider

Rudy never doubted that his dad loved him. His father's mere presence in his life made Rudy different from many of his friends in the neighborhood. "I had that unique experience very few of my neighbors had, and that was that my dad was identifiable. He was present. I had a father who came home. One who spent time with me. He talked to me a lot. He taught me. Many—perhaps most of the other kids in the neighborhood—didn't have the kind of relationship I had with my dad, if they ever saw their dads at all."

When it came to business or bouncing around ideas for something his dad was planning, Rudy's dad would ask his opinion. He was seven years old when his dad started asking him to share his thoughts. "He'd call me Big Shot, Boss Man, and Mr. President," Rudy recalls with a measure of fondness. "Those were my three names, and he would use them interchangeably depending on the situation. If we were having a business discussion, he would call me Boss Man. If he was just hyping me in a conversation with friends, he would call me Big Shot. If he was getting an opinion such as my take on the world, he would call me Mr. President. So between all of those various titles, I always felt appreciated."

Many of the people Rudy met when he took to the streets with his dad did not have much. Life was hard for them, but Rudy's dad made sure that his wife and child lacked nothing. "I grew up being trained as a hard businessman," he reflects. "I never wanted for anything growing up. I didn't miss a meal. I didn't miss a toy. I didn't miss anything material. Everyone in my neighborhood was struggling—everyone. So what I learned to do was hide my privilege. My dad always had at least three streams of income. He always had a job and at least two hustles. He was very industrious and made sure my mom and I were okay—better than just okay."

Therapy has helped Rudy understand his dad better. He's been doing the emotional work to heal aspects of his upbringing that created anxiety, doubt, and fear. Over time he's learned to understand his parents' challenges, which were based on the difficult and unhealed life experiences both of them brought into the relationship. Still, he says, "When I think about love, I wish my dad would have loved my mom better." The material things he brought home were ways to express love, but he wishes his dad had loved his wife enough to leave everyone else alone. Love would have been devotion to his wife, his son, and his home instead of the streets.

Can You Miss What You Never Had?

Rudy's relationship with his dad was close, in one way, but it lacked the intimacy that comes with affection. His father was a practical man, and a gifted entrepreneur, and he taught Rudy a lot about business. Like his dad, Rudy is gifted in the art of the deal. He founded a neighborhood coffee shop, completed over $70 million in housing development projects to provide housing opportunities for the previously homeless, and founded a nonprofit that provides an array of services for families in peril, including distributing fourteen tons of fresh produce weekly and offering HIV testing and services to families impacted by the COVID-19 pandemic. In addition to these ventures, Rudy founded an FM radio station.

His dad believed that if the money was alright, then everything was alright. That approach to life doesn't require affection. "From childhood into my young adult life, I had never been hugged by my dad. We always shook hands." Rudy received affection and hugs from women in his family. He was hugged by his aunt and grandmother, but that was the only touch he experienced growing up. "I only imagined, as a teenager and through my young adult years, what it would have been like to be hugged by him. From the time I was nineteen to twenty years old we were business partners in every venture, and there were always handshakes—no hugs."

Rudy didn't have a frame of reference for how hugs from a father would have made him feel cared for emotionally. Naming the value of something that doesn't exist is hard, if not impossible. Rudy puts it simply: "You can't miss what you never had."

He didn't know the emotional value of affectionate touch until his father gave him a hug, which didn't happen until he was thirty-six years old. "I had become a Christian two years earlier at thirty-four," Rudy recounts. "After becoming a Christian, my worldview started changing around affection. It started shifting around love, and what it meant. I had never told my dad I loved him. I didn't hear him tell me, and I had never said it to him."

After Rudy's understanding of love began to shift, he took the risk of approaching his dad and doing something he had not modeled. "So one day I told my dad, 'I love you.' He responded, 'I love you too.' We hugged."

Rudy shakes his head as he tells me the story now. "It was the craziest thing, man. I said, 'Damn.' I just hugged my pops, and in that moment, all the distance from over the years passed. Even all the stuff in the past—well, that crap just melted."

Rudy's life took a major shift in his thirties, and at first, that shift had a negative impact on the relationship with his dad. When Rudy became a Christian, and he and Juanita started a church, the tension between Rudy and his dad began to bubble over. His newfound faith meant that some of the businesses Rudy's father was grooming him to run—businesses with questionable morality and ethics—were no longer things he was willing to do. Rudy told his dad that he could no longer take money from the family businesses because the money had blood on it. His dad thought he must be losing his mind. What else could explain why someone would walk away from such an impressive income?

Rudy had expected his dad to be happy that he was changing his life for the better, but what happened was the complete opposite. His dad began to tell his friends that he had lost his son to God. His father distrusted pastors and churches, and he resented Rudy for feeling uncomfortable about being a part of the businesses. His father wrote him off as being too weak to get things done anymore and Rudy felt terrible.

Rudy wanted his dad to see that he was becoming a better person—but that wasn't the case. "My dad had a totally different worldview," Rudy reflects. "He felt you became a better person by making some more motherf*cking money. That's the bottom line. So when I think about quality time, I wish my dad had embraced my change. It would have given us the chance to spend time together in new ways that didn't include business."

Conversations between Rudy and his dad had always been about business. When his dad wanted to talk, instead of calling and asking how he was doing, he would call and ask Rudy's thoughts about a business.

Starting a church with his wife was taking a toll on their finances, and Rudy was no longer making the kind of money he had been as a businessperson and hustler. Rudy's dad began to treat him like he was the enemy, and it hurt deeply. For the next three years, Rudy and his dad didn't talk very often. Rudy and Juanita's energies focused on serving and nurturing the church, and his dad stayed away.

Then the unexpected happened.

When Dad Embraces Change

Out of the blue one Sunday morning, Rudy's father showed up for the eight o'clock service at their church. Two years later, he gave his life to God and changed his life.

The relationship between Rudy and his dad began to change. The quality of their interactions improved. Everything was different because Rudy and his dad had both changed. In previous years, their arguments had bordered on violence. Rudy leans forward as he is talking to me; it's clear that he wants me to grasp the gravity of what he's saying. "You have to understand how significant the change was between my dad and me," he says. "He gave me my first gun when I was sixteen. He gave me some rules for using that gun. Rule one was if you pull it out, be prepared to kill the person in front of you. Otherwise, don't touch it. This is not something to scare people off with. This is something you kill people with. That was the rule."

Rudy pauses to make sure I'm with him, and then continues. "When we would argue in those years, though neither one of us would reach for our gun because of the rule, we argued pretty feverishly. My wife was always concerned for our safety. But after I gave my life to God, I stopped arguing. Then after *he* gave his life to God, everything changed. Our conversations, our relationship, and our lives together were better."

Seven years after giving his life to God, Rudy's dad was diagnosed with heart failure and doctors predicted that he likely had a very short time to live. Those were the most intense and loving moments in their lives together. The last night of his father's life, Rudy's dad was in a hospice bed and had file folders scattered all over the sheets. He worked every day right up until his last one.

"I was getting ready to leave and he said, 'Hey, Big Shot. Take it easy, okay?'" Rudy says. "I said, 'Yeah, man,' and he said, 'I'll see you later.' That was it. He was gone after that."

Rudy tells me, too, about his wife's last conversation with his father, which was poignant and searching. The day before he died, he asked Juanita a question that she had likely been asked before, as a pastor, but perhaps not quite in this form. Rudy smiles as he tells the story: "'Baby girl'—that's what he called her—'Baby girl, now this shit you all have been talking about, this eternal life shit: Do you really believe that?'" Juanita, who called Rudy's father Dad, responded, "'Yeah, Dad, I believe it with all my heart.' He said, 'All right, if you believe it, I believe it.' The next day he died."

Rudy and his dad had several really good years. He finally heard his dad say he was proud of him. He finally received a hug, and he saw his dad's values and ethics begin to change. A lot of healing took place over those years, Rudy says, and their story ended well. "As a matter of fact, when we closed one of our businesses—one of the ones that was the most damaging to society—we converted that building to a drug treatment facility," Rudy says. "The guys who ran that facility asked us to come over one night because they wanted to give us an award. It was a room full of addicts living in the building for recovery drug treatment. They gave us an award and asked my dad, 'Mr. Rasmus, what do you want to say?' He said, 'I want to say that I finally found a pastor I can trust.'"

Takeaways

Rudy's "I Wish My Dad" story is the epitome of the way that fathers put to use the old adage *Do as I say, not as I do.* Rudy's father wanted everyone else to live by a code of loyalty, honesty, and fidelity, but his own relationship to those values depended on whether he was at home or on the streets. The complexity of Rudy's father is rooted in his own childhood trauma. Rudy's father likely developed an emotional numbness to cope and to protect himself from further pain and disappointment.

Emotional numbness can turn into a fear of intimacy. The fear of intimacy for Rudy's dad may have looked like chronic cheating, occasional meanness, and being authoritarian in the household to create safety and security for himself regardless of what it cost others. Deceit and secrecy are how he conducted intimate partnerships with family because that's what was modeled for him; loyalty and honesty are how he conducted business relationships and friendships. This contradiction creates a level of cognitive dissonance and is symbolic of trauma. The fear of intimacy may have looked like shaking hands with his son when a more intimate touch, like a hug, was needed. Intimacy requires vulnerability—and why be vulnerable if it sets you up to experience pain and disappointment?

Rudy learned a powerful lesson in his thirties: sometimes sons can be the model for their fathers. Rudy's choice to leave the streets and to dedicate his life in service to God and others modeled for his father what life *could* look like. Rudy's father first interpreted Rudy's decision as just one more person leaving him. But Rudy's steadfastness in his new way of living was so powerful and transformative that his father ultimately made a similar choice. That created space for reconciliation, intimacy, and vulnerability to be present in their relationship.

Rudy modeled consistency for his father, as well as loyalty, integrity, and honor. He became his father's pastor. Rudy's intentionality—to heal his story, to make the powerful and costly choice to transition from the streets, and to go to therapy—has shifted the paradigm of fatherhood and what it means to be a husband. It shows up daily in the ways he loves his wife and fathers his adult children.

CHAPTER 12

I WISH MY DAD PUT FEELINGS BEFORE FINANCES

SIMON

Simon is a lifelong learner. He asks questions and is curious about people—not just about their current stories, but their history. Whenever Simon and I talk about challenges I am facing, he references what he knows about my history and asks if it has any impact on how I am feeling. That's the kind of guy he is: a thinker and a processer, someone who genuinely tries to understand the world.

Simon and I can spend hours talking, and we have honest and sometimes difficult conversations. The key to our friendship is trusting that no matter what either of us says, we say it with genuinely good intentions and a desire to understand. When our conversations are about race and racism, this trust becomes extra important.

Simon, who is white, has lived a very privileged life. I give Simon permission to ask uncomfortable questions about my experiences as a Black man in America, and he gives me permission to give him my unfiltered perspective. He sometimes tells me that he doesn't know as much as he'd like about Black history or the diversity of Black experiences, and he wants to learn. Guided by his Christian faith, he genuinely wants to add value to the lives of others and to society. He is retired, at age sixty-seven, and he and his wife, Joyce, have five children, four of whom are living. At this point in his life, his journey is all about healing and loving others.

"I was raised in a gentrified world of duty and honor, in a Southern aristocratic kind of world," Simon says. "Dad was a pleasant man, and regarded as a gentleman, and I was taught to be a nice boy." Simon's dad wasn't the kind of man who yelled when he was angry; his emotions were more contained. His father didn't have to say much for Simon to know that he was displeased—and Simon never wanted to displease his dad. He held his father on a pedestal and viewed him the way others did: as a highly respected gentleman, scientist, and businessperson.

He and his dad spent a lot of time together, but Simon never felt like he knew his dad because he was so emotionally guarded. "None of who he was or what he was teaching me to be required feelings," Simon reflects. "I knew what he expected from me, but I didn't really know him."

A Dad Defined by His Upbringing

To understand the kind of man Simon's dad was, you need to begin with where he was from. Our environment always has a significant impact on who we become, and Simon's father's context was one of wealth and privilege, as well as one of grief and a sense of abandonment. His father's family owns a lucrative company, a fact that shaped the man his father would become. "It's very hard to talk about the man without talking about the business," Simon says.

Simon's grandfather was an alcoholic and died when Simon's dad was thirteen years old. Simon's father was then raised by his paternal grandparents in the South, and he spent summertime with his mother and maternal grandparents. Simon's dad was very much an outdoorsman, hunting, fishing, and even wrestling with alligators. "You know, all those kinds of things," Simon says with a smile. Simon's father's grandfather was his true father figure, and before too long, he lost him as well. After his grandfather had a stroke and died, Simon's dad no longer had a father figure in his life.

After graduating from college with a zoology degree, Simon's dad went to work for the family business. He was a silent young man who worked hard. Simon's dad eventually became president and CEO of the family-owned company. At the time he saw himself as a big fish in a little pond. Simon's dad liked being known. He served on the boards of other companies and was well respected as a businessperson. He functioned well in elite, aristocratic society.

Simon's dad was a very cordial and pleasant man who didn't like confrontation. Simon and his siblings knew not to push boundaries, because at a certain point he would blow up. But most of those who knew him considered him a gentleman, cordial and pleasant.

"It's odd that I don't feel like I ever really knew the man he was outside the context of business and high-society life," Simon recalls. "What I do know is that as a child I was afraid of him. He never hit me. He never abused me. But I was afraid of his wrath."

In many ways, from an economic perspective, Simon's family lived the kind of lifestyle many people dream of attaining. Simon had access to anything he wanted ... but what he wanted *most* was access to his father. And that eluded him. "I didn't know him through conversations. He was distant as a father," Simon recalls, even though they spent time together.

"Quality time with my dad, if you could call it that, was watching him check on things and maybe talk to employees. From that point of view, I had a lot of time with my dad, but I'm not sure I would call it 'quality time,' because for me that would have included conversation. And that didn't happen."

Simon didn't feel connected to his dad or seen by him. "I remember being in his office and having salespeople come in to talk to him about equipment and packing supplies," Simon remembers. "I would be sitting at his back desk, coloring and doing homework. So again, I was *with* him, but I don't really have a sense of knowing him from that time."

Simon says the times he felt seen and heard as a child were usually when he was with other adults, especially "people who didn't live in our elite social bubble." For example, he felt known by James, who took care of things around their home and drove him to school. "He would talk to me, and I enjoyed our conversations. In some ways I think he knew me as well as my dad did."

During our conversation, Simon searches his memory, trying to find examples of a time when he and his dad actually had a conversation. He has lots of stories of the two of them spending time together—his dad taught him a lot, such as how to hunt, but it didn't require getting to know or understand him. "It was interesting being in a hunting blind with him," he reflects. "It was cordial and pleasant, but time in the woods was silent. It wasn't time to get to know him or for him to get to know me; it was quiet. He wasn't big on sharing about himself. It was more observing and learning—and I learned a lot."

Simon shares a story about how his dad taught him to spot a deer in the woods. One day when they were driving through the woods, his dad asked if he saw the deer in the distance. Simon didn't see it. His father told him, "You are looking *at* the woods. There is depth to the woods. Can you look *into* the woods?" Simon squinted as his father continued. "Separate the trees and the bushes. Try to look beyond the trees and the bushes." By looking into the woods rather than at them, Simon was learning a different way of seeing. Following his father's advice, he finally caught sight of the deer.

It's a fond memory for Simon, although not without irony. The life lesson his dad was teaching him—about looking beyond the surface to find deeper meaning in things—has stayed with him over many years. Yet Simon's dad seemed unable to see into his own son. He often had his son with him, but he never really took the time to be attentive, to look beyond the surface and truly see his son. He never figured out how to understand his son or to see the man he was becoming.

The Ghosts of Duty and Respect

Simon's upbringing was preparing him for a certain aristocratic way of life. "Early on I really began to realize that I didn't fit into that world, although I didn't really fit in the blue-collar world either," he reflects. It was among the blue-collar employees who worked for the family business that Simon felt seen and valued. He grew up around their families and played with their kids. He wasn't one of them, but he felt comfortable among them. They knew his family owned the company their parents worked for, but none of them treated Simon like an outsider to their world. He was embarrassed by their kindness to him, and by his family's power.

Mr. Sampson (everyone called him Mr. Sam) was Simon's Boy Scout troop leader. "I felt like I was raised in his house," Simon recalls. "When it was time to cut the grass, I cut the grass with his boys. When it was time to go to his grandparent's house in the country and they were butchering hogs, I was butchering hogs right there with him. Mr. Sam didn't treat me any differently than his boys." When Simon's dad died, Mr. Sam was at the funeral. Simon saw him leaning up against a tree. He went over to Mr. Sam, buried his face in his shoulder, and wept.

"Mr. Sam was my father figure," Simon says. "I wasn't sure if my dad loved me, but I knew Mr. Sam did." His voice softened. I could sense Simon's love for Mr. Sam as he told the story and reflected on their relationship. They had a bond, and it was clear that he still misses Mr. Sam. "I think my father was driven by the ghosts of duty, and the ghosts of respect, and the ghosts of fitting in. In the Sampson family, I didn't have to do that. There was no expectation to put on a performance."

Simon recalls a story from one of the last times he saw Mr. Sam before he died. One of his sons called Simon to let him know that his parents were coming by and that they wanted to see him. Mr. Sam and his wife arrived at Simon's home, and they sat in the living room to talk.

By this time Simon had been fired from his role as vice president of the family business. The situation was too complicated to go into detail here, but Mr. Sam had heard rumors and wanted to know the real story from Simon. "I told him the story," Simon recalls. "Mr. Sam looked at me and said, 'Simon, I like the man you have become. I'm glad you don't work for the company anymore.' He said if I had kept working for the family business, he seriously doubted that I would have become the honorable man that I am today. He told me, 'The business would have required a compromise of your values.'"

Simon tears up when he recalls Mr. Sam's words now. "'I like the man you have become,' he told me. I wept. I can tell you this: I never heard those words from my father. It's what every son wants to hear from his father."

Needing Dad to Let Down His Emotional Walls

Like all sons, Simon longed to feel seen, heard, and valued. Simon wanted to know his dad beyond the business and social life that he lived. He wanted to be held and affirmed by his dad. All these things were missing.

As we've seen in several of the fathers we've gotten to know in this book, opening up emotionally happened late in life for Simon's dad. He was in his seventies and Simon was in his fifties when his dad said "I love you" for the first time. When Simon was in his thirties, his father did begin to say that he was proud of Simon—but even then, Simon says, those words were attached to what Simon was *doing* rather than who he was *becoming*. "He said, 'I'm proud of you. You have bought and sold more houses than I have, and you have moved more than I have.' So he was proud of me for making my way in the world. He was proud of my activity. I never really heard him say anything like I heard Mr. Sam say: 'I'm proud of who you have become, your character.'"

One man, his father, saw value in what Simon was doing in the world and affirmed him for that. The other, Mr. Sam, saw who Simon was becoming in the world and affirmed that.

About five or six years before his dad died, Simon had an encounter with his dad in which he felt that his dad was finally beginning to see and value who Simon had become. On that particular day, Simon was visiting the family home to pick up some of his things. During the day he, his dad, and other family members were at the swimming pool, grilling. Simon was sitting with his dad while everyone enjoyed the pool and other activities. They sat together not talking, as was typical for them.

But this time his dad broke the silence. "He said, 'Simon, you're a good listener. Have you always been a good listener?' I said to him, 'I've been listening to God a lot these last two years, and it is a lot harder to listen to God than to people. God has made me a good listener.'"

His dad took in that information for a bit, and Simon and his dad walked back toward the house to check on the grill. Then his dad began the conversation again. "He said, 'Simon, can anyone pray?' I said yes. He said, 'I don't know how to pray.'" Simon paused and looked me in the eye. "My father had never asked me questions like this. It was like I was getting an eye into his soul, an eye into who he was. Then my dad asked, 'How do you pray?' I said, 'Well, you just start talking to God, like you and I are talking right now.'"

It was the kind of conversation Simon had so desired to have with his dad—one that moved beyond business and into an intimate space of sharing. Simon shakes his head at the memory, still marveling. "My dad said, 'Maybe one day you will teach me to pray.' I said I would love to."

It was just a glimpse into his father's vulnerability, a brief conversation in which they both shared personal thoughts, but it was a milestone in Simon's relationship with his father. Simon says, "It was a miracle. God transformed my anger into this incredible love for my father."

Money Is Not Love

Simon and Joyce's third daughter Sarah was born with profound disabilities. It was a normal pregnancy and delivery, but Sarah started having seizures when she was a month old. She died when she was six years old. Her death was roughly six months after Simon's mom died of emphysema. That same year Simon's dad had open-heart surgery. It was a rough year for the family.

During that time, his dad was living in the family home by himself. Simon and Joyce cooked gumbo and took some to his dad. "So we brought him some frozen gumbo and before we left, he said, 'Wait a minute, Simon. I have something to give you.' He came back with a very large check. He looked at me, and he gave it to Joyce and me, and he said, 'Money is not love, but it is the best I can do.'" It is clear as Simon tells the story that Simon is reliving it and feeling the emotions the same way he felt them on that day years ago. We sit in silence for a minute, and I tell him it is completely okay to cry. He takes a breath, sits back in the chair, and continues as I listen.

Simon tells me he wanted to tear the check up in front of his father. He was so angry that he wanted to cry. Simon needed love at that moment—a hug, some words of consolation, an expression of love and care—but instead, his dad offered him a check. The family was experiencing so much loss and sadness, but his dad couldn't open up. As I listen to Simon's story, I want to weep: for Simon, for his father, for all the ways that fathers fail to console and enter into their children's pain.

Just as Simon always wanted his dad to take an interest in who he was becoming as a man, on that day he needed his dad to take an interest in his pain and sadness. Even if his dad couldn't find the words, the power of his touch would have made a difference. "I wanted him to hug me and ask how I was feeling. Even if he was not willing to let me into his feelings, I wanted him to come into mine."

Learning to Forgive and Love Dad

Simon has done a lot of emotional and spiritual work that has allowed him to forgive his dad. He's now aware that his desire to be seen, valued, affirmed, and loved were valid. Simon has come to understand that his dad was unable to open up. Simon's dad was not nurtured in an environment that taught him how to share his feelings or take an interest in the feelings of others. Simon understands all of that now, and it has helped him release his father from those expectations. "He wasn't able to give me what I needed, and I forgave him," he says. "The needs I had then are needs I still have now. Today they are being met not by my dad but by my wife and others." He credits his wife, Joyce, with helping him feel loved in the ways he longed for.

Simon has a deep and abiding faith as a Christian, and he also attributes his ability to forgive his dad to God. "I began to see him for who he was, and I had to give him the space to let him grow in that," Simon says. "In the last couple of years of his life I began to see a softer man, a man who did hug. In the end he began to see me, and I am grateful for that."

Simon has now learned an important aspect of parenting adult children: that is, inviting your children into your pain without bleeding on them. He has learned to share his story with his children while working not to impose his past pain on them. "I am trying to come to grips with my faults so that I can love them the way they need rather than expecting them to live up to my expectations the way my dad did to me."

Simon is learning to be gentle, quieter, and less opinionated with his children. He is honest, too, as he reflects on the ways he wishes he had been a different father. "I can easily see how I have fallen into some of the same behaviors when it comes to putting too much attention on what they do rather than loving them for who they are," he says. "When I look at their character, values, and how they treat people, I have every reason to be proud of who they are—and I am," he tells me. "I have parented through my brokenness. Today I continue to ask God to show me those places that still need to be healed and redeemed."

Takeaways

Simon's "I Wish My Dad" story is filled with generational expectations and demonstrates how family businesses can disrupt relationships between fathers and sons. Growing up with rigid family expectations, sons can't follow their own pathways of discovery but must align with familial desires to safeguard the family brand and business. Simon's dad fell in line with these expectations and found himself the CEO and president of the family-owned business. I wonder what dreams and desires Simon's father sacrificed to fulfill familial norms. I wonder how his passion for wildlife would have evolved if he had been presented with an alternative pathway of self-discovery.

Simon's father raised Simon the way he was raised: to quiet his desires, silence his dreams, and engage in a type of performance that limits self-expression. A culture that values what is on the surface and what one does to earn a living will always eclipse the fullness of being human. This way of being in the world makes more room for teaching rather than talking, for performing rather than knowing, for restricted engagement rather than storytelling, hugs, and "I love yous." Simon's desire to be known beyond his productivity led him to find the son-father relationship he desired in his relationship with Mr. Sam. Mr. Sam and his family provided an environment that made Simon feel safe enough to be authentic.

Simon disrupted the generational pattern—of aligning with familial expectations—when he was fired from his position in the family business. This was a difficult moment for Simon, but the job termination ended up creating a freedom that enabled Simon to find a pathway that worked for him.

Sons who can let their fathers off the hook for not meeting their expectations make room for forgiveness. They eliminate the destructive ways anger sits in the mind and body. Simon's heightened self-awareness, and his intentionality around healing, has strengthened how he parents his children, and his choices now free his own children to offer the same healing to future generations.

CHAPTER 13

I WISH MY DAD TOOK RESPONSIBILITY FOR HIS MISTAKES

ROB

I met Rob after my first book was published. Not only had he read the book, but he invited me to his home so that I could meet several of his close friends. He had purchased copies for all of them, and I immediately realized that this guy is a very kind and generous person. He has a heart for seeing people heal from trauma and live better lives. He's a loyal and supportive friend, always checking in to make sure everything is okay and offering whatever he can to help.

Rob, who is fifty-seven and married to Karen, is a family man who loves his wife and children. He's a proud girl-dad, and his two daughters are everything to him. He spends time with his daughters talking, having fun, and listening to their stories. Offering his daughters hugs, words of encouragement, and quality time, he is being the dad that he always wanted.

Like many sons, Rob carried the tremendous weight of unresolved trauma from his childhood for many years. When he was young, Rob's mother took him and moved from Oklahoma, where they had been living with Rob's father, to Washington, DC. Rob was in his twenties when he first reconnected with his dad. He was in the military and had just returned from Germany, he tells me. When Rob returned, he had a chance to go back to Oklahoma. He was a twenty-year-old soldier with an attitude.

What comes next may not make a lot of sense to you now. But trust me when I say that it will, after you read Rob's story in the pages ahead. As Rob tells me the story of going to his father's house as a young man, he leans forward in his chair. "I arrived at his house and rang the doorbell," Rob tells me. "Then I punched him in the face and walked off."

When Dad Is Abusive

When Rob talks about his dad, the first memories he shares are of his father abusing his mother. "I literally have an image in my head that I carried for years: my father beating my mother bloody," Rob tells me. He recalls a fight between his parents when he was four years old, during which he ran over to his mother's side as she stood in the kitchen. Even at that young age, his impulse was to try to stop and even absorb his father's violence. His presence did not stop his dad, who continued to beat Rob's mother. "I jumped on him and he kicked me off, kind of threw me into a wall. My mother grabbed me, picked me up, and took me to another room in the house."

As a result of the fight he witnessed, Rob's mom lived with a scar on her chin. That night his father had knocked out a number of her teeth. She had to have major dental work—reconstructive surgery—that left some pretty bad scars that impacted her for life. This was the imagery Rob was left with from childhood of the kind of man his father was.

His mom began working overtime to save her money, and two years later she moved herself and her son from Oklahoma to Washington, DC. She only told one person where they were going. "My mother was incredible," Rob says. "She was loving. She was spiritual. We prayed our way through all kinds of ups and downs, as she faced all the challenges of being a single mom in an urban environment."

Rob grew up running track and playing baseball and football. He would get upset that his mother had to take him to practice. It was an experience he wanted to have with his father. His friends on the team had their dads; some were coaches and very involved with their sons' lives. "If we were playing football, they were going through drills with their dads. They were playing baseball with their dads. I never had that. I always wanted it," he says. He believed that the kids whose fathers spent extra time with them throwing the ball around and pushing them a little bit harder after practice were the kids who had more confidence. "If my dad had loved me and shown me how to love, I believe I would have been more confident in myself," he says. "I may have had better natural talent than some of those kids, but I backed off in competing against some of them. I felt that I couldn't compete with them since they had their fathers." Rob pauses. "I had a lot of insecurities about not having a father around to help me."

Having his dad present to support, coach, and encourage him in his interests would have been what love looked like for Rob. He missed a father's presence and guidance. "As a preteen, there were so many decision points, and a lot of times, I didn't make good choices," he reflects. "I wish my father could have been there to show me love and guide me."

Rob shares his dad's name, so he is Rob Jr. He has often resented having to carry his father's name because of the memories he associates with it. "I couldn't wait until I grew up so I could change my name," he says. Sometimes family members told Rob that he reminded them of his dad, and he would get angry, assuming it was a criticism. But people in Rob's family had a different perspective of who his father was, one that didn't align with what he had experienced. His cousin Henry, for example, loved Rob's dad and spoke highly of him. Henry had been abandoned by his own dad at a young age. Rob's father, who lived close by, would sometimes take him fishing or hunting.

Rob still seems a bit baffled when he tells me what Henry told him when they had both reached adulthood. "Henry said my father would come get him early in the morning and take him out, making sure that he had food and that he had money," Rob says. Rob was angry as he listened to his cousin share stories about how helpful his dad was and the role he played in his life. "I was totally upset," Rob tells me. "Henry looked at me, though, and he said, 'You know what? Now I get it. After all the years, I couldn't understand why Uncle Robert favored me, but now that I look at you in stature—we look alike. We actually do. Out of all my relatives, we could pass for brothers.'"

Rob pauses for a moment as he recounts this conversation. "Henry said, 'You know, Uncle Robert was probably doing things for me because you were not available, and he couldn't do things for you.'" At that moment Rob viewed his father from a different perspective. Now he was willing to get to know the Uncle Robert everyone was so fond of and spoke so highly about.

Renewing Connection

To sum up Rob's relationship with his father while he was growing up would be to try to put words to an absence. In a conversation about their own fathers, Barack Obama and Bruce Springsteen describe absent fathers as "ghosts." They talk about coming to terms with their fathers' absence in their book *Renegades: Born in the USA*. "Ghosts are deceptive because you are measuring yourself against someone who is not there," Obama says at one point. "And in some cases, I think people whose fathers are not there, and whose mothers are really bitter about the fact that their fathers are not there, what they absorb is how terrible that guy was, and you don't want to be that guy."

Rob felt like his dad didn't care because he didn't spend time with Rob or provide any financial support. In fact, Rob never heard from him. Given all this, you may have a better understanding of why a young soldier would search for the father who had abused his mother and punch him in the face.

As Rob got older, he wanted not only to let his father know how angry he was; he also wanted to know *who* his father was. Somewhere within those six or seven years after punching his dad in the face, Rob had begun to rely on his faith. He became less angry and had a desire to know more about his dad. He started calling his dad, and over time they cultivated a relationship. Rob had matured, and his perspective was now guided by his faith. He was still angry, but hearing stories like Henry's told him that his father wasn't always a mean and abusive person. Rob always wanted the image he had of his dad to change, and stories like Henry's gave him hope that it could.

Rob began taking trips to Oklahoma just to be around his dad. He always hoped his dad would have the conversations with him that he needed to heal. "The conversation I was looking for was something like, *I'm sorry for beating your mother. I'm sorry for not being there.*"

While Rob continued to reach out to his dad, there was always something beneath the surface that he was hoping would happen: an apology, or even an acknowledgment. On one occasion his dad was in Maryland helping Rob build his house. Rob had grown comfortable with their relationship. After hanging some drywall, they called it a day and went out for a glass of whiskey and cigars. As they sat together drinking and smoking, Rob decided it was time to have an honest conversation.

"I want to know why you beat my mother," he asked his dad. "Why did you beat my mother? You beat her bloody."

Rob's dad had become a Christian by this point. He felt that Christian values would have allowed his father to see the pain he caused and feel remorse for his action. But what his father said next revealed more than he likely knew: "You're married," his father told him. "You know what kind of relationships men and women have. That's all I'm going to say about it."

Rob felt like his dad's response was a slap in the face. "Dude beat my mother! All of the stuff that she has gone through. I wanted to hear: *I'm sorry. I was a different person then, I'm a Christian now and I have better values.*" Rob gets angry now as he recalls the conversation. An apology from his father would have been a pathway to healing for Rob. If his dad had been willing to own his mistakes and say he was sorry, the pain could have eased for both of them.

Afraid of Affection

Rob struggles with the idea of what affection could have looked like from his father. We have hit the most challenging part of our conversation, and I can tell that talking about receiving affection makes him uncomfortable. He sits back in the chair across from me, wringing his hands and looking down at the floor.

"Affection is a hard one for me, just maybe based on different experiences that I've had in life," he says. It's clear to me that something has been triggered in him—a memory, perhaps. The way Rob talks about affection suggests he still thinks it's unmasculine. The moment I mention affection between fathers and sons, he wants to clarify what appropriate affection between men looks like. But I am not talking about men in general; I am asking about his dad. Rob has a fear of men showing affection to each other, and I want to know more.

"When I was a kid, I had a newspaper route, and there was one customer who invited me in," Rob says. "He tried to . . . to . . . become affectionate with me. I was maybe twelve or thirteen years old, and I didn't have anyone to talk to about it."

Let's stop here in Rob's story for a moment. It's clear that the man on his paper route wasn't trying to be "affectionate"; he was trying to molest Rob. But when men don't have precise language for emotion, we often lack the vocabulary for other things that happen to us, including abuse.

Rob is my friend. I love him like a brother, and I can tell he is carrying something that he has never given voice to. I've learned that pain begins to lose its power when we give voice to it, and I want Rob to speak his pain. I want him to begin his process of becoming free from it. So I press on, asking Rob if there is a more accurate way to describe what happened to him in that house. He is clearly uncomfortable, shifting and turning in his chair. Frustrated that I am pressing him, Rob answers, "He was trying to molest me as a man. I guess that is how another man would show affection."

I interrupt Rob. No, this is not how a man expresses true affection, I tell him. Affection and sex are not the same thing. Molesting a child is a criminal act. As a young man, he lacked the language or experience of true affection, and he lacked the language to distinguish between real love and abuse.

I tell him: the man on his paper route attempted to molest him. But it wasn't affection—in fact, it was the furthest thing from it. I tell Rob that I am sorry that happened to him.

Rob tells me that he got out of that house. The man left him alone after that dangerous encounter. "I said I was going to tell my mother and I was going to tell the police," Rob says. "I cussed him out. I said, 'No. You're not going to put your hands on me. Open the door and let me out.'"

Rob hadn't talked to anyone about it until now. But the story left an indelible mark on Rob's understanding of affection. That day took something from Rob. It took away his ability to give and receive affection and to disconnect it from sex. From that point forward, he couldn't think about affection without that day serving as his reference point for touch.

Rob deserved to experience affection without fear of harm, I tell him. He deserved to experience hugs, a kiss on the cheek or forehead, and the words "I love you" from his father.

Admitting We Needed Dad's Love

Rob is still finding it difficult to describe what he needed love to look like from his dad. I ask him the question a few different ways, and I can tell that the questions are frustrating to him. I can hear the tension in his voice, and I can tell that he really doesn't want to say he needed his dad for anything, and that he still holds anger toward his dad because he abused Rob's mom.

Thinking about the love that he offers his own children, Rob simply can't fathom a world in which his dad could do that same thing. That may be true. But the question isn't about what his dad did; it was about what he, Rob, needed. Just because he didn't receive it doesn't mean that he didn't need it or deserve it. "I made up my mind that since my father wasn't coming around, then he wasn't going to be the person I needed for anything," he tells me.

These days Rob hugs his daughters as a display of love and to convey, through compassionate touch, that he is there for them. With some pressing questions from me, he finally admits that in an ideal world, he would have experienced the same thing from his dad. Still, giving voice to what he needed is frustrating to him. "I don't want to go there," he tells me, and I appreciate his transparency. "He is dead and gone, and I still have to deal with it, whether or not I was able to receive affection from him. What am I going to do with it?" There is silence in the room, and we sit there for a moment as Rob begins to cry.

Rob is right, in a way. His dad is not here anymore and wishing that things could have been different with his dad doesn't change the past. He is never going to hear his dad say "I love you." He's never going to receive a compassionate touch or a hug from his father.

But this is a conversation about owning our longings and about giving voice to our needs. It's about those things that a son has desired to receive but never had a chance to talk about. It is about naming a son's needs to feel love and connection. Because while his dad is now gone, the needs are not.

Rob and I have a good but hard conversation about what he needed from his dad. He wrestles with even admitting that he needed things from his dad. It's healthy to be honest with what we need even if the person we wanted to receive those experiences from isn't here. It keeps us from carrying the sadness and pain. It's a way to let go of any lingering resentments that do not serve us well. Naming what we needed is a lens into identifying what we *still* need now, as adults.

As Rob's friend, I want him to be honest about what he needed so that he can free himself from the weight of holding it in. Rob's childhood experiences were real, but they don't have the right to define affection in his life through the lens of pain and abuse. It's also okay to admit to wanting that from his dad. As Rob has revealed, there is a lot tied to even the word *affection* for Rob. "I hate the word because I don't know what the hell it is supposed to feel like from a father—what he is supposed to share affectionately with his kids, with his son," Rob says. "I didn't know affection. I didn't know how a man was supposed to show affection. I hate that I missed out on that experience from my father."

That's it, I think to myself; that's what I have been waiting to hear from my friend. I thank him for naming it, and he continues. "I wish my dad had spent quality time with me as a child," he adds. "I always wanted to hear him say 'I love you. I'm here for you. I am proud of you.'"

Rob is now able to see that he still has needs and that he can allow himself to receive support from others. Rob is blessed to receive love from all the above. He has two amazing daughters, Jazzmin and Sheridan, who love him dearly. He offers love to his children in the ways that they need it: through hugs, saying I love you, spending time in ways that make them feel loved and valued, and being present in moments when they need the support of their father. In offering them what they need, he also receives what he needs. They hug their dad, tell him how grateful they are for him, hang out with him when he goes fishing, and are just present with him during peaceful moments at home. Sometimes the void is filled by friends, a spouse, and even our children.

Rob is getting the love he has always deserved. He didn't receive affection from his dad, but he receives it now, from his wife and daughters and me and other friends who hug him and tell him that we love him. He knows that he is safe with us.

Takeaways

Rob's "I Wish My Dad" story is filled with numerous adverse childhood experiences. Rob holds his experience of violence in his body. Research shows that one in six boys are sexually abused by the age of sixteen. Although Rob was able to escape his victimizer, the imprint of the violation persists in the ways he thinks about affection, particularly with men and specifically with his father. It is not uncommon for boys who are sexually or physically abused to become men who have difficulty discerning the differences between affection, sex, abuse, love, and nurturing care. It is a gift that Rob's mother was able to move away from her abuser, to relocate with her own and Rob's lives intact.

How do sons avoid carrying the anger and resentment when they have been victims of violence, especially at the hands of a parent who is expected to love, nurture, and protect? It is no surprise that Rob's trauma response, upon seeing his dad after many years, was to punch him in the face. It is a blessing that despite this interaction, he and his father were able to have some semblance of a relationship. It is heartbreaking that Rob's father presented a lack of remorse for abusing Rob's mother when Rob confronted him.

Rob's dad's response to being confronted—*You're married. You know what kind of relationships men and women have*—indicates that he likely also witnessed domestic violence and was experiencing unresolved trauma of his own. Trauma can change the structure and chemical functioning of the brain. Rob experienced this answer as unacceptable. Rob's dad had not done the work to heal his own trauma. When we tuck away the pain points of our lived experience, it is very difficult to acknowledge the pain we have caused someone else.

Rob has chosen to heal in an effort to learn how to parent from a healthy place. Rob's choice to engage in therapy is powerful. He now has a better understanding of his own trauma, which also gives him a better understanding of what his dad possibly experienced as a child. This awareness doesn't mean he now makes excuses for his father's behavior; it simply means he has a better frame for understanding who his father was.

CHAPTER 14

I WISH MY DAD WAS VULNERABLE

JORGE

Jorge and I met officially at a conference where he and I were both speaking. He had heard of me, and I had admired his work for years. Jorge pastors a church in Cape Coral, Florida, that has an amazing range of ministries including substance abuse recovery and empowering people with different abilities. Jorge is committed to helping people confront and heal their own stories so they can thrive. Jorge is also a mental health advocate. He has his own therapist and will gladly tell you why every leader should have one.

In addition to being a pastor, Jorge is an author, coach, husband, father, and loyal friend. He's the kind of guy you can count on to show up in a pinch. The way he loves his two children, who are now adults, is a beautiful thing to see.

For my final interview, I fly down to Cape Coral, Florida, to interview Jorge about his dad. Barefoot and wearing a T-shirt and shorts, Jorge greets me at the door with a laugh and hearty hug. "My brother! Welcome, come on in!" He has already started making dinner. Grilling by the pool overlooking the lake, he's preparing steak and an assortment of other meats. After dinner, we sit down to talk. As Jorge shares his "I Wish My Dad" story, he refers to "the family business" and how he was fortunate enough to get out of it.

Curious, I ask him to explain, as I can sense that there is a story under the story. I want to hear Jorge narrate both the story on the surface and the story underneath. As we talk, Jorge tells me about his father, their relationship, and the business from which Jorge had to free himself.

The Work Ethic of Two Men

Jorge describes his dad's story as "what the American dream looks like." His dad is now ninety-three years old and lives in Florida. Jorge's dad is the oldest of six siblings, raised on a very poor farm in Puerto Rico. Along with his mom and dad, he helped to take care of his younger siblings. Working on a farm, going to school, and providing for the family meant a lot of hard labor.

Jorge's dad joined the military as his way out of poverty. He served for twenty-five years in the US Air Force. He was a jet engine mechanic and then he became a flight engineer, which put him in the cockpit of B-52 bombers then the C-141s and the C-5As, the jumbo transport jets. He received the distinguished Flying Cross, which is the third highest medal in the military. He went to Korea, to Vietnam, and then, in retirement, he even went to Iraq as a civilian contractor. "I sometimes say that, at ninety-three years old, he would suit up and go if they would take him," Jorge says with a smile.

After serving in the military, Jorge's dad started his own business. He purchased an air-conditioning business and did very well financially. "I remember the day the red Cadillac with the white roof showed up," Jorge recalls. "The one thing Dad wanted to have was a red Cadillac. Mom and Dad would take trips to Europe. For three years his company was breaking records in sales."

Business was thriving until the recession of the 1970s hit. The oil embargo and the halt of construction projects damaged business for Jorge's dad. He tried to keep the business going, and he spent his entire personal fortune to pay his employees. During this time, he didn't take a salary. He tried to see it through to the very end, hoping to survive the recession, but the business didn't make it.

"I remember the day the attorney showed up and put the home in my mother's name," Jorge recalls. "My dad sold the Cadillac, and he went to work at a convenience store as an evening cashier. I was in high school at the time. I remember looking in the glass windows and seeing my dad mopping the floor."

Losing his business during the recession knocked him down, but Jorge's dad got back up. He learned that he could go to Iran and work as a civilian, training jet mechanics. As a contractor for the US government working in Iran, he rebounded and made a second fortune. He came back to the United States and then went to Saudi Arabia for several years. He continued to travel all over the world, and his business and wealth were solidified once again.

His dad took care of the family financially, and Jorge is grateful for that. More than provision, however, Jorge and his family needed presence. Giving of himself emotionally would have been more valuable than anything he could buy. Jorge had access to anything he could have ever wanted, but the thing he wanted most eluded him: the presence of his dad, both physically and emotionally. Meeting the emotional needs that Jorge had as a child would have required his dad to show up differently. He would have needed a broader lens of what it meant to be a provider.

When people think of provision, it's typically through the lens of things: both necessities and luxuries. A broader idea of provision, however, can include providing a violence- and anxiety-free environment. Provision for one's family can include providing safe space for emotional expression without judgment or the fear of rejection. Jorge wanted his dad to be as generous with his presence as he was with possessions.

"He once told me his greatest fear in life was being poor because he grew up poor," Jorge tells me. "From working on a farm to the military, owning a business, mopping floors, to bouncing back and succeeding again, Dad had the work ethic of two men."

A Paradox of Love and Anger

While Jorge's dad was a hardworking and successful businessperson, his story as a father is far more complicated. As our conversation pivoted in the direction of his father's parenting, Jorge leans back in his chair and begins to explain. He recalled coming across a letter that his dad wrote to all his kids. He wrote it in 1969 while in Vietnam.

"It is interesting that until a number of years ago my personal remembrance of my dad as a father and that letter were miles apart," Jorge tells me. "In the letter he begged for forgiveness for being away from us to serve our country, and how he wanted to make it up to us when he came home. For most of my young adult years, my personal narrative was that the bad choices I made in life were a direct result of my dad's inability to be at home when I was a kid."

Yet Jorge's perception of his father at a young age didn't necessarily align with reality. His father's absence from the home, due to military service or other work, wasn't the hardest part of life with his father. "My dad took up what I call 'the family business,' which was drinking," Jorge says. "Our family has a history of drug and alcohol addiction. My father told me a story of when he was a young man. He was near his grandfather's—my great grandfather's—home. My dad picked an orange off the tree to eat it, and his grandfather, in a drunken stupor, pulled out a gun and tried to shoot him. For picking an orange!"

His dad's grandfather was an alcoholic; his dad's father was an alcoholic. His dad is an alcoholic. Jorge and his brothers also took up the family business of alcoholism. That's four generations.

When his dad wasn't there, Jorge's home was fairly peaceful. But when his father was there, it was inconsistent. When his dad was drinking, Jorge and his siblings didn't know what to expect. If the drinking led to his dad being angry or mean, things got ugly, and there was lots of screaming, yelling, and cussing. "I have a vivid memory of him being very angry with me, chasing me with his belt and spanking me," Jorge says. His memory was of dad who was absent, and when he was present, he was angry.

Yet sometimes he was a happy drunk. His dad traveled the world and would come home with nice things like pineapples from Hawaii, pistachios from the Middle East, and other unique items. In public, especially, he presented as a happy, jovial kind of person. But at home Jorge didn't want to make him angry. "The metaphor that feels right is walking on eggshells," Jorge reflects. "It was never safe—and by 'safe' I don't mean that he was going to physically hurt me, although every once in a while, it did involve getting whipped. But home was never emotionally safe."

There was always the threat of being yelled at or walking in on arguments. Jorge recalls what it was like growing up in his parents' home and sometimes compares it to what home was like for his own children. Comparing the safe space that he and his wife created for their children to his own childhood brings back sad memories. When his kids were young, their friends would come over and he would join them, building forts, playing tag, and bringing out hot dogs. Jorge realized that when he was young, he didn't get to have those moments with his dad.

"One day when my kids were young, my son Nathan asked if one of his friends could spend the night. I said, 'Absolutely, we'll have a great time!' Then I immediately wondered if anyone had ever spent the night at our house when I was growing up. I called my mom and asked. She said, 'Oh, no. We never had kids spend the night because we never knew what condition your dad would be in.'" Jorge pauses. "That's what I mean by unsafe: we never knew what to expect."

Jorge's dad's letter from Vietnam told a different story: one of a loving dad, separated from his family by circumstance. Jorge's dad was much better at writing how he felt than he was at expressing his feelings through how he interacted with Jorge and his siblings. It's almost as if the father he wanted to be came forward in his writing. But he couldn't figure out how to set that gentler, kinder version of himself free. The letter told part of the truth. "But for me he was both: loving and angry," Jorge says simply.

Dad Never Laid Down His Armor

It took having his own family for Jorge to realize some of the things that he missed out on with his dad. Knowing what he knows now—about what fathers can be for their children, and what a father's simple presence can mean to a child—he realizes what he didn't have.

When Jorge was growing up, his family took lots of vacations. They would go to Puerto Rico to see family every chance they could. But more often than not, Jorge and his siblings were just with their mom because his dad was flying. His dad would meet the family at their destination because he was gone a lot. At the time he didn't know what he was missing not having his dad around on trips. Jorge points to an area in his living room across from where we are sitting.

"We have photo albums over there that are just filled with pictures of the vacations my wife and I took with our boys. We're talking about trips to national parks, the Grand Canyon, Yellowstone, and Disney World. But when I look back at trips I did with my mom and dad, the memories are different, because he wasn't always there, sometimes physically and never emotionally."

"I wish my dad loved us by letting himself be fully known. I think machismo [a traditional Latino idea of manhood] is about a false front. Never let them see you sweat."

Jorge always loved sports. When he was in the eighth grade, he played flag football. One day during a game, he hit a guy across the helmet with his hand. Pain shot through his arm, and he walked off the field holding his arm gingerly. He went up to his father and told him that he thought he had broken his arm. "He said, 'Go back in and play—don't be a pussy.'"

Jorge cringes as he tells the story, remembering the pain. "So I went back in and played the game with a broken arm. When I got back home, I said, 'Daddy, it hurts. I need to go get it checked.' He said, 'No it's not. Go to bed.' I went to bed, but I was up all night in pain." The next morning Jorge's arm was really swollen. His father finally took him to the doctor, who said the arm was broken and put it in a cast.

On that day when Jorge broke his arm, he needed his dad's protection and affirmation. Even after realizing that his son had been right, his father never said he was sorry. He didn't take care of Jorge on that day. "I wish he had believed me," Jorge says. "I needed to be taken care of at that moment. I was thirteen years old. I needed him to be my protector."

Fathers can be present physically—showing up for games, attending concerts—but not truly present. Being present requires entering a son's world as a participant, not a spectator. Seeking to understand him. Seeing who he is becoming and affirming his value. Listening to what he cares about—his fears, hopes, and dreams—and then offering loving encouragement.

"I wanted my dad to be emotionally invested in learning about me," Jorge says. "I think part of parenting is becoming a student of your child. It's saying, 'What brings you joy and delight? And how can I engage in that with you?' That's what I wanted: for him to be curious about me. I think that if he had been given the gift of self-awareness, he would have been able to offer love in ways that our family needed instead of focusing on himself." An extreme level of self-care can be one outworking of unresolved trauma. When you need to protect yourself in times of danger, focusing on your own safety and well-being at the expense of others' can become a habit.

I know other men like his dad who were soldiers during the Vietnam War. My dad was one of them. He has some of the same emotional issues as Jorge's dad. I also served in the army during the Gulf War. One of the ways some soldiers deal with what they saw or experienced is by not dealing with it at all—never talking about it, except perhaps with other soldiers. The walls created by veterans' silence tend to keep the pain in and people out. Sometimes our goal is to just get by in life without falling apart. But it's hard to see the emotional damage that that armor of invulnerability does to loved ones.

"My dad saw a lot in Vietnam," Jorge tells me. "He had emotional walls up and didn't let us in. Throughout my childhood, we got this kind of facade. He was the provider. He was the American hero. He was all those things—the successful guy. But being a dad in the ways that we needed him, beyond money? That was missing."

Jorge's dad was a soldier. He understood battle, survival, strategy, discipline, fear, courage, and resilience. Those were some of the things required to make it home. He applied both the skills and training from the military to becoming a successful businessman. But the military didn't train him to be a dad. After twenty-five years of service, like a warrior, he had grown comfortable with wearing his armor.

Jorge and his family needed him to put his armor down, love his family, and allow himself to be loved in return.

The Inner Need for Connection

Throughout my conversation with Jorge, he talks about an inner need that, as a kid, he didn't always have a word to name or describe. He just knew something was missing. He was desperately desiring *something* from his dad, but he didn't know what. "I don't always remember what I was feeling, but I do remember the feeling and thinking, 'This is all kinds of wrong.' I didn't know what the relationship with my dad was supposed to look or feel like, but I knew that what I was feeling wasn't it."

Jorge was conditioned to believe that love looked like a bag full of gifts from world travels. Deep down, however, he knew the gifts were not filling the void or speaking to that feeling he was unable to name at the time. The true gift he wanted to receive was the gift of his dad being present, open, and available.

Jorge shares another memory of his dad returning home from Vietnam after a twelve-month tour of duty. The family was living in Puerto Rico at the time. They knew he was coming home, so the family went to the airport, sat down, and waited as soldiers were coming off the plane. Jorge was ten years old. He sat looking down the stark green hallway, watching men in their fatigues come in and wanting to catch a glimpse of his dad. Seeing his father come into focus, Jorge ran down the hallway toward his dad. Sobbing, he threw himself into his father's arms. Dad was home.

"Even though he was a pretty absent father who seldom, if ever, took off the warrior armor, I still needed him desperately," Jorge says. "I still wanted an emotional connection."

For a brief moment that day, he received what he needed: the warmth of love that came from jumping into his dad's arms and being held. It was a primal response that allowed him to put aside the fear and the anger for a loving embrace. It was moments like that Jorge wanted more of.

Relentless Love

In the sunset of his life, Jorge's dad is much more willing to be vulnerable. He talks about what he is afraid of with his son. He opens up and shares his feelings. "The man I know now in his nineties is in some ways very different from the man I grew up with," Jorge tells me. "There is a tenderness about him now." The man he is now is the father Jorge needed growing up.

Some things have changed for Jorge's dad since he became a Christian. Faith has softened him and made him more affectionate. These days when Jorge and his father talk, the conversations are more open. His dad shares his feelings, and he's a bit more like the man he was in the letters he wrote than like the man his kids feared.

There are still times when his dad tries to pick up his armor, but Jorge is able to lovingly help him set it down. His dad still isn't very self-aware, but Jorge is and that allows him to love his dad with grace and forgiveness.

"There has been a redemptive part of our father-and-son story," Jorge says. "As I've done my own work to heal and become more self-aware, my capacity to love him is back. I am able to give him what he needs even when he can't give me what I need. I think that's how love has to look sometimes."

Jorge has two adult sons, Daniel and Nathan. He works hard to affirm them without attaching it to performance. His sons are not afraid to hug and hold their dad because he has created a safe space for affection. He doesn't always get it right, but he loves his kids for who they are and does his best to offer love the way they need it.

"I genuinely see my sons with love and affection," he says. "They are people to be loved and not a problem to be solved.

When they were young, I was a performance addict and imposed that on my kids. But today, performance is not the filter for how I love my boys. If I had to describe how I love them now, it would be relentless love."

Takeaways

Jorge's "I Wish My Dad" story is of a father who was unable to offer full presence due to his own experiences of childhood trauma, trauma incurred while serving in the military, and machismo. Jorge's father's use of money to communicate love was his way of protecting himself from the risk of intimacy and vulnerability. Money is never a substitute for presence.

Living an integrated life requires us to fully feel joy and pain without resorting to numbing agents. A father's willingness to fully accept himself and engage in the work of healing creates space for a son to also be vulnerable and learn how to accept his full humanity. Jorge's father created an unsafe environment for his family when he used alcohol to hide from the things in his life that also made him feel unsafe. The pain points he attempted to hide from showed up in the tension, yelling, and emotionally reactive arguments with his wife, which left long-lasting imprints on his sons. Having the courage to confront pain releases power within us, and ultimately, we begin to feel safer in our skin.

Somewhere along the way, Jorge's father learned that men should always be able to bear pain and tough it out. His statement, *Go back in and play—don't be a pussy*, to his son with a broken arm illustrates this. To every father and son: it is an illusion to believe that you have to choose suffering and pain over your wellness. You deserve your wholeness.

It is a blessing that Jorge can experience more vulnerability and emotional presence from his father in this late season of his life. Jorge's relentless love for his own sons, detached from how they perform, speaks to his ability to be self-aware. His self-awareness will nurture new healing patterns within his sons and future generations. Emotional safety allows everyone to take off their armor and be their vulnerable selves.

CHAPTER 15

I WISH MY DAD SAID "I LOVE YOU"

ISAAC

Isaac is affectionately known by most people as "Pop." The epitome of a gentle giant, Isaac is retired and spends most days hanging out at his daughter's restaurant. Isaac is a great storyteller. I love listening to him share stories: from graduating from high school in Arkansas in 1963, to moving to California with six dollars in his pocket and a whole fried chicken, to making history as the first African American to serve in the top supervisory role in the Los Angeles City Street Services, a role that had him supervising more than one hundred people.

Indeed, at seventy-seven years old, Isaac is known for his stories, which he frequently shares at the dinner table with family and friends. Many of his stories revolve around growing up as the son of a sharecropper in Arkansas—and around the hardworking, kind, and honorable father who raised him.

Isaac speaks fondly of his dad, from whom he learned a lot about life and hard work. He and his eight siblings knew they were loved. But the words "I love you" were not frequently spoken in his home. Many fathers I've met tell me that when it comes to love, actions speak louder than words.

I decide to ask Isaac what he thinks. Would hearing his dad say "I love you" have made a difference to him?

Son of a Sharecropper

Isaac's dad was a hard-working man, dedicated to the well-being of his family and his faith as a Christian. He did the best he could to provide for his family as a sharecropper in the segregated South. Interviewing Isaac gave me a chance to hear about share-cropping firsthand, from someone who did it. He explains to me that as a sharecropper, his dad—along with Isaac and all eight of his siblings—worked on another man's land. His dad would receive 50 percent of what the land produced. They would provide the labor: the planting, tending, and harvesting of the crops. The landowner would receive the other 50 percent. Sharecroppers never knew exactly how much the crops sold for, however, because they were not present when the crops were sold. The very nature of sharecropping caused Isaac's family to live in debt.

Isaac wants to make sure that I have a clear understanding of how difficult it was for a sharecropper to provide for a family of ten, so he offers an example. Say he and his siblings had worked with their dad to harvest fifty bales of cotton. They would have no way of knowing what those fifty bales sold for, and would simply have to take the word of the white landowner. White landowners were often only one or two generations removed from men who thought owning Black people was moral. "The landowner may have said, 'I got thirty cents a pound for the cotton,' but he may have actually gotten sixty cents a pound," Isaac says. "You had no way of knowing. We just had to accept his word and go on from there. Some years we raised a lot of cotton, but we never really got out of debt."

Everything had to be harvested by November, before winter set in, because the crops would die during the winter months. Work came to a halt in December. "All during the winter until harvest time next year, you were allotted a certain amount of money," Isaac tells me. "In other words, you borrowed money from the owner of the land to live each month. Generally speaking, it was the white man who owned the land. We would borrow money from him, whether it was $100 or $200 a month, to get us through the winter. When harvest time began, the initial harvest went to pay off your debt." Isaac's dad would not receive the 50 percent due him until *after* the winter debt had been repaid. He says that in addition to planting, growing, and harvesting the crops, his dad had to pay for the cotton seeds they planted on the owners' land with his earnings. Every year, then, was a punishing cycle of hard work tied to a cycle of insurmountable debt.

Planning ahead was essential in making sure the family had everything they needed to get through the winter months. Isaac's dad taught him how to hunt and fish so that the family could store food for the winter. He and his dad would go fishing in the summer and hunting during winter. "I got to be really good with a peashooter because I was hunting for food," Isaac says with a smile. "Everything I hunted for was food for us. My mother would stock the freezers."

Isaac's family raised their own chickens, hogs, and other animals for food. They would buy flour, beans, and seasonings with the loan from the landowner. To this day, Isaac still applies the lessons he learned from his dad during those years of sharecropping. He has several freezers full of food in his home. He doesn't hunt anymore, but he still enjoys heading out to a lake not far from his home to go fishing. When he prepares meals, they are reminiscent of those that he grew up eating in his childhood home.

His father instilled the values of hard work and always doing what is right and honorable out of respect for the family name. Isaac's dad was always present in the home and as a farmer, and his children worked alongside him to care for the land. He and his siblings always knew where their dad was. As a man with a fourth-grade education, he taught his nine children what he knew, and what he knew was farming. So all of his children learned how to make a living growing their own food and the skills they would need to survive during hard times.

Living within the dehumanizing context of sharecropping in the segregated South, Isaac's father managed to instill an ethic of kindness and honor in his children. "Do unto others as you would have them do unto you" was a core principle that Isaac and his brothers learned from their dad. He raised them to be kind young men of strong character and values, and hardworking men who provide for their families. When they were kids, Isaac and his brothers never went looking for trouble, because they knew that if they did anything to dishonor the family name, their dad would not be pleased. They respected their father and wanted to make him proud.

"We grew up with that strong belief that we had to look out for each other," he says. "We had to be kind to each other and kind to everyone and always know our family was our responsibility."

Quality Time with Dad

Isaac's dad made time for all nine of his children. He and his siblings grew up during a time when there was no television, so they spent a lot of time together playing games like checkers or softball or just talking. Sometimes Isaac's dad would take the boys outside, draw a line down the street, and race them to see who would finish first.

One man in the neighborhood—the Candy Man, as he was called—would drop off candy for Isaac's mom to sell. He would come back in a month or so to collect the money, and Isaac's mother would get to keep some of the candy in return for selling it. "After working in the field with my dad, he would say, 'Okay, it is time for us to quit for the day,'" Isaac recounts. "As we headed home, we would get about a hundred yards from the house and my dad would say, 'I'll bet you a candy bar I can beat you home.'"

Isaac shakes his head and laughs. "He would beat us every time." By the time he and his brothers got to the house, their dad would be sitting on the porch, waiting. He'd smile and point them toward the candy box. To fulfill their bet, they had to buy the candy bar from their mom for their dad. Eventually, after they'd lost both the race and the bet several times, they realized they just couldn't beat their dad.

From time to time, Isaac's dad would gather his children together to teach them about their family history. Some of their ancestors were enslaved, including his mother's father and his great-grandfather. "My dad would sit with us, and we would talk, and he would explain to us life as a whole to the best of his knowledge: how to treat people, how to get along with people, how to grow this, how to grow that."

Isaac's dad expressed love through his actions. "I don't remember Dad saying words like 'I love you' too much," Isaac reflects. "But he showed it in so many ways. I guess hearing him say it would have been good, but he didn't have to say it for us to know that he did." His father expressed love for his wife and children by being a provider and spending time with his children. Yet hearing a father say "I love you" is special. It's empowering for children, and in a way that's often hard to describe.

Isaac also wishes his dad had hugged him more often. Isaac recalled being hugged on his birthday, but hugs were not a routine way to express affection in their family home. "I think I would have welcomed more hugs," Isaac says. "If he had hugged me more often, it would have been another thing to help me grow. I had plenty from my dad, but that would have been the icing on the cake."

Isaac leans forward, elbows on his lap and hands clasped. I have the sense that he is about to share a story. He begins to describe his days as an athlete. Isaac played baseball and was a very good pitcher. One year his high school team went to the state championship. Unfortunately, it was an away game, and because they didn't have enough money, his dad could not go to the championship game.

Isaac was his team's star pitcher, and he was having a great game. In the ninth inning it was close, but Isaac's team was winning. Runners were on first and third base. A batter Isaac had struck out several times in the game came to the plate. He knew what pitches to throw in order to strike him out again. As the batter approached the plate, Isaac's coach walked out to the mound and told him to change the kind of pitches he was planning to throw. Isaac knew his coach was making a bad decision, but he listened to him anyway. He threw the first pitch in the way his coach advised him to throw. The batter swung and got a base hit; the runner from third base scored, and Isaac's team lost the state championship.

Losing his last high school baseball game hit Isaac hard. He walked home from the game discouraged, carrying the second-place trophy. When he entered the house, his dad could see the sadness in his eyes. "My dad told me what a good job we did as a team and all that kind of stuff," Isaac says. "But a good, strong hug would have been really great. I wanted to feel the strength of my dad. He had always been there, but that would have been the time for a strong hug."

The power of a hug can never be underestimated. Like Isaac said, it's the icing on the cake of a father-son relationship.

Making Dad Proud

Isaac had earned several baseball scholarships when he graduated from high school, one of them to Mississippi State. But it was 1963, and there was a lot of racial tension related to school integration. Simply attending school could be very dangerous for a young Black person, so the decision about college was not easy. Isaac was aware of another student who attended school in Mississippi. He wasn't welcomed and had to be escorted on campus by the National Guard. "There was so much racial tension going on down there that I declined to go," Isaac reflects. "I was an Arkansan, and I had dealt with enough racism. I didn't want to go to Mississippi and deal with more, so I gave up the scholarship."

Having passed up a college scholarship, Isaac knew that he did not want to be a farmer like his dad. Isaac told his dad that he would not be around to bring in the next harvest. Unsure about his future but wanting to explore new opportunities, he decided to head out West. He'd move to Los Angeles in search of work so that he could help support the family.

Isaac's first job was washing cars on Ventura Boulevard. He had to drive forty-two miles one way to get to work, and he made sixty cents an hour. Even with his limited wages, however, Isaac could keep enough money to live on and send the rest home to help his dad provide for the family. It was a selfless act of love, and Isaac's dad appreciated it deeply. "My dad looked upon me in a different way because I got things done, and because I could figure out how to do things without anyone having to tell me," Isaac says. "I always remembered the family I left behind, and I was always doing things to support them."

From the car wash, he went on to take a job detailing cars. After that he bused tables and washed dishes at a country club. From there he went on to clean hotels and drive-in theaters. Isaac was a hard worker, and he simply did whatever he could that would allow him to send money home.

After a few years living in California, Isaac was drafted, but the military messed up his paperwork and ended up sending him to Germany, where he served for two years. At the end of his enlistment, Isaac returned to Los Angeles and started assembling the wing of the military "Phantom Fighter" used in the Vietnam War. Then he worked on the wing of the L10-11. As the war was coming to a close, he kept getting laid off because the military required fewer planes.

I imagine that Isaac didn't realize it at the time, but in all his jobs—from washing cars and busing tables to being in the military and building fighter planes—he was stumbling in the right direction. He was accruing experience all along the way. Just before he was about to be laid off, Isaac had applied to and passed the test for a position with the city of Los Angeles for a maintenance labor job. He took the job with the city, and that decision changed everything.

From maintenance laborer—the lowest classification in the city bureau—he moved up to become a light truck driver, driving sanitation trucks and street maintenance vehicles. From that job he moved up to driving a heavy-duty water truck, and then to driving a city street sweeper truck. With every promotion, he was moving up to a higher-paying position within the city. As a result, the amount of money he was able to send home to help his dad and the family increased. After driving a street sweeper for a few years, he passed a test and was moved up to a supervisory level. "Instead of sweeping streets, I was in charge of getting those streets swept," he tells me.

Isaac advanced to the highest rank possible for anyone with a high-school diploma to achieve in working for the city of Los Angeles. He was the first African American to attain the position of Superintendent II and oversaw a team of 260 people. He worked for the city for almost thirty-three years before he retired. He had lived the leadership role his dad saw in him, his fourth-born son.

Isaac's father passed away when Isaac was working as a light truck driver for the city. He didn't witness his son's full career journey firsthand, but he was always proud and let Isaac know it often.

"I know my dad would have been in his glory seeing my outcome and the things I had done with what he instilled in me," Isaac says. "I wish he could have seen that his hard work paid off in how I lived my life. I'm grateful for everything he taught me.

He may not have said he loved me, and he didn't hug me very often, but what he had to give he gave in full measure."

Hearing the Words "I Love You"

Isaac's dad was present for him and his siblings. He taught them how to work hard, provided for the family, built strong character in his children, and even raced his sons for candy bars.

But I still want to know if hearing the words "I love you" would have had value for Isaac. So I ask him the question I've been wondering about during our entire conversation: would hearing "I love you" spoken out loud have made a difference to him as a son?

As I press Isaac on this question, he sits back in the chair, legs crossed, and tilts his head back. After a brief silence, he responds. "Yes, seeing or hearing him say things like that would have made me a little bit stronger. In starting my own family, I knew that I would have to do the same thing. It would have been easier for me because I would have already been trained to say, 'I love you' more often."

For Isaac, knowing that someone cares and *hearing* that person say "I love you" are different things entirely. "It may be quite thrilling just to hear those words sometime," he reflects. "Those words are comforting, and they are words people would love to hear more often. I told my dad I loved him more than he told me. He told me how he *appreciated* me."

We might know someone loves us, but hearing those words makes us feel better and stronger. There is power in simply hearing "I love you."

Takeaways

Isaac's "I Wish My Dad" story is filled with the inspiring legacy of a family two generations removed from slavery in the segregated South. Slavery functioned—and still functions via the prison industrial complex, as Michelle Alexander and others have pointed out—to break the spirits and identities of those enslaved. Slavery is an effort to create profitability and wealth for those who align with the illusory identity of whiteness. Those of the African diaspora—the enslaved and now their descendants— were never meant to thrive. Isaac's family, who constantly lived in debt due to the nature of sharecropping, is evidence of this. Debt disallows one to access opportunities for wealth building, particularly the ownership of land and property.

It is a miracle that Isaac's father was able to render the harshness of slavery and the unfairness of sharecropping into survival strategies for his nine children. Instead of passing on trauma, he passed on lessons in kindness and strong character and the honor of the family name.

I imagine that Isaac's father's stories highlighted the strength, courage, tenacity, and boldness necessary to live within a culture of slavery and racial hatred. His stories instructed his children in the strong lineage they had. I wonder what trauma Isaac's father held in his body even as he was being fully present with his children in working, playing, and storytelling. I wonder if using the words "I love you" and initiating hugs more often would have penetrated an aspect of him he was trying to protect. Growing up, he had to cope with the threat of losing his family at the hands of a white racist at any moment. I wonder if *he* was ever told "I love you," or given hugs by his father. Parents often parent in ways modeled to them.

It is clear that Isaac experienced the loving warmth of his father despite the lack of hugs and "I love yous." This propelled Isaac to have the courage to create a life for himself and his family that exceeded what the systems of slavery and sharecropping intended him to have. It is his father's principles about manhood—having good character, cultivating strong faith, operating in kindness, and being a provider—that enabled Isaac to rise from maintenance laborer to the highest position someone with only a high school diploma could hold in the city of Los Angeles.

Isaac's father cultivated a confidence and knowingness that conveyed to him who he was and *whose* he was: God's child, one having intrinsic value and worth. Fathers like Isaac's dad ensure their sons know their identity, so they will not look to their peers, the media, and societal constructs of worthiness to feel validated.

CHAPTER 16

I WISH MY DAD GAVE AS MUCH TO ME AS HE GAVE TO THE MOVEMENT

KAMASI

Kamasi and I share a love of art. Both of us collect paintings from across the Black diaspora. Kamasi is well versed in African American history and the way that identity and politics have shaped who people believe they are and can become in the world.

Kamasi loves young people and is inspired by students who have a passion for learning. He teaches high school students and is also a filmmaker, author, and documentary producer. He doesn't just care about young people getting a quality education; he cares about the kind of people they are becoming. Kamasi encourages his students by speaking to their academic ability and by affirming the good he sees in them.

Learning the story of his dad gives me a much deeper understanding of where Kamasi's commitments started. His father was deeply committed to causes of justice and equity. Kamasi and his dad had wonderful conversations while Kamasi was growing up. Those conversations covered three topics: Blackness, identity, and religion. Those were his dad's interests, and they subsequently became Kamasi's interests. As an adult, Kamasi has added in movies and music.

The conversations between fathers and sons have a direct impact on sons' intellectual identities and trajectories. As a young man growing up and trying to figure out who he was, Kamasi was deeply shaped by those conversations. Yet he also experienced emotional neglect, and an authoritarian father who likely believed that this way of raising his son would safeguard him from the harshness of life that he had experienced. He experienced a father who gave sacrificially to an important movement for Black lives. The immense amount of effort and energy Kamasi's father gave to the movement prevented him from seeing that his son and family needed his emotional presence and investment.

What if fathers could see caring for their families as an act of political engagement?

Watching Dad Evolve

Kamasi was born when his dad was in his early twenties, and like many sons born to young fathers, he was able to observe his dad's growth over the years. The oldest of four siblings, his dad had grown up on a farm in Martinsville, Virginia, during segregation. Shaped by rural, Southern, and Protestant sensibilities, many members of his father's family were farmers and preachers. He explained that for his dad, this meant a very strong ethic around labor. You wake up every day, work hard, and prove to everyone—and to God—that you are a hard worker.

By the time his father was seven years old, Kamasi's grandparents had moved the family to Detroit. This was toward the end of the Great Migration, as many Black families moved to Northern cities from Southern states where Jim Crow reigned.

So while his father spent his initial years on a farm, he spent his formative years in the city.

Detroit was a fascinating city for a young Black boy whose parents had a sixth-grade education. The man he became in Detroit was shaped by Black politics of the 1960s and by the racism that limited opportunities for young Black men no matter where they lived. He barely graduated from high school and began working for Ford Motor Company. He went to community college, and he was also seduced by drugs. Various social streams were shaping his identity as a young man, including Black radical politics.

When Kamasi's father got off drugs, he became a Christian. In his twenties and thirties, people knew him as a young father and a person interested in Black politics and Africanism. By the time he was twenty-five, he was attending Harvard Divinity School to obtain a master of divinity degree.

No matter what stage of life he was in, Kamasi's dad was always working. He is known for many things, but the dominant theme in his life is work. The work ethic that began as a child in the rural South never left him. "He's always been driven," Kamasi says. "A farm boy turned scholar turned preacher, he has always been working. When I was growing up, he always had to have something to work on. He always had to have a project. He's seventy-three years old now, and he has published over fifteen books. He has preached in every major country in the world and lectured at some of the biggest universities."

The only time Kamasi would see his father laugh or be playful was when he was watching a movie or listening to music. "My fondest memories of my father are of him going into his office and playing jazz while he was writing," Kamasi tells me. "He would have his head down with his yellow pad on the desk and pencil in hand. To this day, he writes everything by hand. When he finished, he would come in the living room and turn on the vinyl—reggae, R&B, and whatever was out. But he was always serious."

As a kid, Kamasi was always a little on edge when he was around his father. He never knew when to interrupt his dad, because he was always working. Kamasi's relationship with his father was shaped in many ways by his father's identity as an activist and scholar. "Being a father and investing in his children was secondary or tertiary at best," Kamasi recalls.

For a very long time Kamasi felt like he was always vying for his father's attention and approval. So many large issues concerning the African American community and oppressed people globally took precedence in his father's mind. These commitments often left Kamasi feeling like he had to compete for his father's attention.

When Kamasi was in the sixth grade, he joined a baseball team because he wanted to get his father's attention. His dad has always loved sports. But ultimately, joining the team didn't work in the way Kamasi had hoped, because his father only showed up for one game.

"I remember the first practice after the day my dad showed up for the game," Kamasi says. "The coach looked at me and said, 'You never threw the ball as hard as you did the other day. You never played that hard. Your father was in the area, and you played your behind off.'" Kamasi looks at his hands as he tells the story to me now. "He was right. I was trying to get his attention."

Being Dad's Main Student

Kamasi's dad was strict and firm, which was his way of keeping Kamasi from straying into drugs the way he had. But he wasn't present for Kamasi emotionally. As much as his dad tried to give him guidance, Kamasi sometimes felt like his father treated him less like a son and more like a professor treats a prized student. "When I was a junior in high school, my father was teaching a course on Black politics at the local university," Kamasi tells me.

"I was doing everything I possibly could to get him to love me and want me. So I would sit in on his class. But I stopped going because the students got mad at me for knowing all the answers. I was like, 'You all need to listen to him!' I remember my dad being very impressed by that. I was trying to get his attention by showing off. I didn't really give a damn about the kids in the class, so I wasn't aware that their ire was directed toward me. It was all about trying to get my dad's attention."

Kamasi wanted to be seen by his dad, but not just as his most prized student. He wanted his father to see him as his son, and he longed to connect with his father without feeling like he was being instructed. Kamasi needed his dad to be nurturing and emotionally present. He needed him to be affirming not for what he does, but simply for who he is.

Kamasi wishes his dad had used language that was more affirming and less intellectual—words that expressed his feelings for his son. An essential component of the politics of the Black radical tradition and movement is love. His father failed to bring the love of the movement that he cared so deeply about into the experience of fatherhood. What if his father could have figured out how to radically love his Black son? What if his father could have invested in his son in the same way he invested in the movement?

Kamasi also wishes his father had been able to apply the curiosity with which he approached scholarship and activism to his parenting. Love does not impose its will, but love is inquisitive. It asks questions like *What do you need? How are you feeling? How can I help?* "I wanted him to be more curious about what was happening with me internally," Kamasi reflects. "I needed love that was observant and curious about me."

"My father never asked me, during the height of the crack epidemic when all of my friends were being shot at or killed, 'How are you feeling? Are you okay? What's going on with you?' The interiority of my own life was not something that either of my parents talked about a lot. I wanted his presence to honor my own identity, to honor my own interiority, to honor and be curious about how I was feeling."

Kamasi was bullied a lot between fifth and seventh grade. Those three years were just brutal for him. But there was never a conversation about bullying from his father. His dad found out about it when Kamasi was in the seventh grade. "All of the adults in my life failed me," he tells me bluntly. "It was obvious that I was being bullied. In the third year of bullying the teacher said to my dad, 'I notice the kids are a little hard on him.' My dad had this look of shock and surprise on this face. There was no conversation about it, or very little. Three years . . . and he was just figuring it out."

If Kamasi's dad had had an emotional investment in his son, he would have noticed much sooner than three years into the crisis. He would have been curious enough to ask questions much earlier. "As a ten-year-old, I didn't know what I needed to hear, but I knew how I wanted to feel," Kamasi says, in one of the most succinct summaries I've heard about what young sons long for. "I wanted to feel affirmed. I wanted to feel like I was of value, of worth. I needed my dad for that, but he was unable to offer the emotional presence I had been desiring for years. He didn't really see me."

Needing a Place to Feel Safe

It was during those years of being bullied that Kamasi joined the baseball team with the hope of getting his dad's attention. What he didn't share initially with me is that he was also being bullied by his teammates. Everywhere he turned, there was no feeling of safety.

Kamasi is ready to share something with me that he has not yet shared with others. I can tell by the way he approaches the conversion with such clarity that he has thought about how to describe what took place before our conversation. "My parents were just as physically tough on me as the world was," he says. "There was no place of safety. I was getting beat by them too. They were physical disciplinarians and very hard on me. So from fifth to seventh grade, my body was never in a place where I felt safe, protected, and affirmed."

This is the first time that he is giving voice to this trauma and naming what he needed. He needed to be seen, and he needed to be protected, and he wasn't. As we continue the conversation, I want to know if there is anything else that he needed as a child. "I needed my dad to hug me," he says. "I was scared of my father, so there was a space of fear. I had to tiptoe around him a lot, so I didn't really feel affection in my house."

Home was not a place of horror, he clarifies, but neither was it a place of peace. "I needed an environment where if I wanted to get a hug, it would be available to me." Kamasi would have had to develop a lot of courage to approach his dad and ask for a hug. "It wasn't something that I ever felt comfortable with because I was always scared," Kamasi says. "I was always scared to ask him for lunch money. The only thing I wasn't scared to ask for was help with my homework. I did have an opening there."

Kamasi was afraid of being rejected. Afraid of his dad saying no or being angry. He pauses to consider what would have happened had he asked his father for a hug. "Now that I'm reflecting on it, I don't think he would have said no," he tells me. "He wasn't a cold-hearted person. But as a child, it never dawned on me to seek it because I never felt comfortable doing so."

Children need entry points to their parents' attention. Kamasi's parents would have needed to cultivate an environment that felt emotionally and physically safe. They would have had to tell him that he could ask for what he needed without fear of rejection or physical threat.

Kamasi wishes his dad was aware that quality time is important. He gave quality time to learning, teaching, lecturing, preaching, and more. His son needed him to bring that same energy and passion home and apply it to raising his son. He wanted his dad to choose his family first, as the number one priority. His dad was about investing his time in movements to bring about liberation and freedom for oppressed people. At the core of fighting for the rights of others is love. Without love it's not a movement; it's just a bunch of activity. Had his dad focused on love as the reason for everything in which he invested his time, perhaps he could have seen his son's need for love—love that affirmed his value and made him feel safe physically and emotionally.

The relationship between Kamasi and his dad has improved. They haven't come full circle to the point where all the issues have been addressed and healing has occurred, but they are more connected, loving, and affirming of one another. They ask each other questions that show interest in each other: *How are you doing? How are you feeling? How is your health? Talk to me about what is happening in your life.* These are conversation starters that allow them to share their truths.

"I still think there are some deeper conversations my father and I need to have," says Kamasi. "There is a part of hurt that is still there. But I will say that our relationship is much better."

Takeaways

Kamasi's "I Wish My Dad" story is of a well-intentioned and committed faith and community leader who was an emotionally neglectful father. Kamasi's father was raised in the segregated South and became politicized as an adolescent during the 1960s. His enslaved ancestors were forced to work beyond exhaustion to generate profit for white slave owners. During this time, Black bodies were commodities whose worth was measured by how much they could produce. Kamasi's father and so many other Black men of his generation inherited this way of valuing their own worth: based on production. This work ethic ended up being both a blessing and a hindrance.

Pan-Africanism, one of his father's commitments, places great emphasis on collective ambition to achieve economic transformation. Sometimes this worldview means the sacrifice of the individual. A parent's commitment to any cause or movement can sometimes cause harm to a family system.

Kamasi's father dedicated his life to investing in his own intellectual and spiritual formation, as well as his blackness. The emphasis on these strands of his identity left little room for him to be the father Kamasi desired. The physical discipline, strictness, and firmness Kamasi's father implemented in his parenting was authoritarian. Children raised by authoritarian parents are generally given little opportunity to voice their feelings and needs.

Kamasi's story invites all men to consider what they may be trying to run away from when they pour sacrificial amounts of energy into work or activism. How do fathers' commitments sometimes take away from the level of emotional cultivation a family system requires? Movements are only sustained through the thriving of family units. Without healthy families, there is no movement. It is the loving investments we offer to our families that overflow to the movement, the church, and other commitments. Our families are our first investments. This notion is challenging for many activists and faith and community leaders.

It is a gift that Kamasi's relationship with his father has improved, and that they are now able to affirm and love one another as they continue to deepen their relationship. Kamasi disrupts a cycle of emotional neglect each day by being a teacher who affirms his students and the good he sees in them. His father disrupts a way of parenting that most likely was modeled for him each time he accepts Kamasi's invitation to dive a bit more deeply into knowing and being known.

CHAPTER 17

I WISH MY DAD GAVE ME MORE OF HIS TIME

ANDY

Andy is the kind of guy who has never met a stranger. He can walk into a crowded room and, in a matter of hours, has talked to just about everybody. Being a part of the community and caring for others make him come alive. His energy is palpable.

Andy is fifty-seven years old, and he and his wife, Rowena, live in Lilburn, Georgia. They have three children: Carlos, age twenty-five; Josey, eighteen; and Ellery, sixteen. Andy is vice president for advancement at a global nonprofit organization.

Andy holds his own father in high regard. As a young man, his father served in the navy as a pilot and then flew commercial planes for an airline. He was a compassionate man, committed to his Christian faith and with a heart for helping people in need. Being a pilot connected him to people globally and gave him opportunities to share his faith.

Andy's father was also a get-things-done kind of guy who kept a busy schedule. He worked full time for the airline, ran a ministry for pilots, founded a church, and served as an elder. When the church was between pastors, he would even take on that role. Andy admired his dad's commitment to so many people and institutions.

But as he describes his father's involvements, I can sense that something is missing from the story. He looks downward for a moment. "My dad was very committed to God's work, which was a beautiful example for us to follow," he says. "But for me, his commitment was a challenge."

Wanting More of Dad's Time

Andy was a talented student athlete who played competitive soccer in high school and college. In all the years he played sports, his father only came to one game. He was used to his dad having a busy schedule, so his absence felt normal. When his mom asked him once how he felt about his dad being so busy, Andy excused his dad's absence and told his mom that it was fine. But in his thirties, after having his own son, Andy began thinking about the kind of father he wanted to be. "I realized that I was carrying anger about the fact that my father only saw me play one game," he tells me now.

Andy's family lived a ten-minute drive from his high school. After home games, the soccer team would head over to the field house to shower and change clothes. Those moments in the field house were somber memories for Andy, no matter whether they won or lost a game. After changing clothes and briefly meeting with the coaches, Andy and his teammates would walk to the parking lot where parents were waiting to take them home. Many of the boys were greeted with smiles, hugs, congratulations, or "Cheer up—we'll get them next time." But for Andy, that was not the case. "I would go get in my car and drive myself home. My parents were never there."

Andy's dad was a huge Georgia Tech football fan. He understood American football, but he had no idea what soccer was about. The anger Andy carried because his dad didn't come to games had less to do with his excitement about the sport and more about wanting his dad to show up for him. If Andy had played football, would his dad have shown up to games? Probably.

But Andy longed for his dad to show up for him, whether he liked the game or not.

Sometimes being present for our sons requires being present on *their* terms and doing what they want to do. When our sons see that we are making sacrifices of our time to step into their world and on their terms, it's evidence to them of our love. It's what love looks like.

The Ripple Effect of Time

To his credit, Andy's dad was an affectionate father, and unlike many sons, Andy grew up frequently hearing his dad say the words "I love you." Andy's dad didn't have a problem expressing his love in both words and deeds.

Whether it was at church or hanging out with friends, the positive energy of his dad's personality would fill the room. That was the same environment he created at home. "Some of my favorite memories of him are from when I was much younger," Andy says. When his dad was home for family dinner or breakfast, the family would sit around the table, all six of them. Breakfast was a big deal, and his dad loved a big breakfast, with more than enough food for everyone. Gathering around the table was a time of laughter and great conversation. Meals usually included people from the church or a missionary from another country who were staying with them for a few months. Their home was always a welcoming place. Those experiences have shaped Andy's spirit of hospitality. Andy is constantly extending invitations for friends or colleagues to join his family for a meal.

Andy's birthday and his dad's birthday were only a day apart. Every year on his birthday, he would sit in his dad's lap after breakfast and have the same conversation. "He would say, 'You're my youngest, and you used to like sitting in my lap. How old are you going to be when you're too old to sit in my lap?' I would always say, 'Another year, Dad, another year.'" When Andy was around twelve, he decided that the tradition of sitting in his dad's lap after breakfast had come to an end. He remains grateful to his dad for taking the time to create memories in his life that still spark joy.

Andy's father hugged all his children often. "If he was heading off for a flight for three days, he would hug us all, kiss us on the head, and say, 'I love you, and can't wait to see you when I get back.'" Andy also saw his dad model what a loving relationship looks like between a husband and wife. He saw his parents laugh together and banter lovingly. "Sometimes Mom would be cooking dinner and Dad would come behind her and give her a hug," Andy remembers. "She would say, 'Joe, leave me alone; I have to get dinner ready.' She would say it in such a funny way." Together his parents created a home that was happy and peaceful.

Always a hugger who said, "I love you," his dad created an environment where his children felt safe to talk to him about whatever was on their minds. At times he shared stories about his travels around the world, and those always fascinated Andy.

Yet even affectionate parents who are busy with too many commitments can leave their children longing to spend time with them. Like many of his generation, his dad also saw the role of being a provider as a way of showing his love. Andy appreciated his words and deeds, but what he valued most was his father's time. For him, that was the greatest experience of love.

Andy is the youngest of four children. His dad was far gentler with his sisters than he was with Andy and his brother. He was definitely more lenient with his daughters. "My brother and I were fine with the love that our dad showed for our sisters. But when it came to his time, I think we struggled with the need for him to invest the same amount of time in us."

Andy always knew that his father loved him, but the lack of his presence had a ripple effect. "Looking back at my faith journey, when I reflect on the idea of 'God the Father' and 'heavenly Father,' my image of what that looks like is tied to the relationship with my dad," he says. Andy says he has sometimes felt distant from God. In Andy's thoughts, if God is like his father, then God must be distant. It took Andy years to redefine his relationship with God and find a healthier approach to his faith that allowed for a more intimate connection with his spirituality.

A Hard but Healing Conversation

About twenty years ago, Andy tells me, he was reflecting on childhood memories: missing his dad's presence at soccer games and feeling sadness and anger about his dad's general absence. The memories hit Andy hard, and he realized that holding on to negative feelings was hurtful. Andy decided that a conversation with his dad was in order if healing was going to happen.

Conversations about past pain require a lot of vulnerability, especially when sons initiate them. Will our fathers listen to our feelings with love, or will we be met with opposition? Will the open wounds of our memories heal as we talk about them—or just reopen? Will we simply get rejected or misunderstood or hurt once again?

Andy tells me that he decided to give it a shot. He was ready to have the conversation. So at age thirty-four, Andy drove home from Nashville, where he was living, to Georgia for a weekend to see his parents. The back of their house had a screened-in porch. After church and Sunday lunch, his dad would make his way to the back porch and read the newspaper.

When Andy arrived, his dad was sitting comfortably in his chair, reading. He walked out back and took a seat across from him. Wasting no time, Andy jumped right in. He started out sharing memories from his days of playing soccer in high school and college.

Andy's voice softens as he recounts the fact that he proceeded to name the source of his pain. "I reminded my dad that in all of my years in soccer, he only saw me play once. I said, 'Dad, I have to tell you, that really hurt me. I am carrying it to this day. I didn't feel like what was important to me mattered to you.'"

After another brief silence, Andy says, his dad began to cry. He explained how he had, in recent years, realized the way that his passion for serving the church had kept him too busy. He explained to Andy that pastors and mentors who prepared him to serve the church had instilled the belief that "you take care of the ministry, God will take care of your family."

But Andy's dad did not make excuses for his absence. "Dad looked at me and said, 'I'm so glad you spoke to me. I've actually prayed and asked God to forgive me, but I didn't know how to talk to you about it.' He told me that he was sorry he wasn't there for me." Andy and his father talked for a couple of hours and cried healing tears together.

Andy had been courageous enough to share the source of his childhood sadness, and his initiative was greeted with loving compassion.

Making the Effort

Andy grew up with a love for hunting and fishing. His father, who grew up during the Great Depression when hunting for food was out of necessity, associated hunting with memories of difficult times. But after their conversation on the screened-in porch, Andy's dad made the effort.

Knowing that he enjoyed fishing, his dad started reaching out every now and then to schedule time for the two of them to go fishing. "He would call me and say, 'Hey, I think it's time we go,'" Andy says. "We would plan a trip once a year and go fishing, just the two of us. I watched him change to do things that he knew meant a lot to me."

Andy's mother developed early-onset Alzheimer's disease in her late sixties. By that time, his dad had retired from the airlines. "I watched my dad care for my mother for ten years," Andy reflects now. "He would take care of whatever needs she had. He fed her, spent time talking to her, and sat by her side until it was time for her to go to bed in the evening. That was his routine every single day." In addition to caring for his wife, Andy's dad would meet with staff at the Fellowship of Christian Airline Personnel—a ministry that he founded—pray for them, and have lunch with one of his friends. The only time in a five-year span that his dad was away from his mother for any extended length of time was when Andy took his dad fishing.

As Andy sits in my office sharing how his dad cared so lovingly for his wife, I see Andy demonstrating the same kind of love and compassion for his own father, who is now in his late seventies. A few years ago, Andy took his dad down to Suwannee, Florida, to go saltwater fishing. It was a hot day in the Gulf, and Andy and his dad were pouring out sweat as they reeled in fish. It was a good day. Andy could tell that the heat was getting to his dad, though, so every so often Andy would dip towels in an ice cooler and place them on his dad like a cold, wet blanket. He leans back in the chair and laughs as he remembers.

The plan was for Andy and his dad to spend two nights away fishing. But a day into the trip, his dad was thinking about his wife. "I remember, as we finished cleaning up the fish, my dad looked at his watch, then looked at me and said, 'You know, if we left now, I could get home in time to feed Barbara and put her to bed.'" Andy got in the truck and said, "Let's go!" "I could tell he just wanted to get back and see her before the day was done," Andy says.

As a child Andy didn't have the words to explain that he needed more of his dad's time. It wasn't until he was in his thirties that he was able to tell his dad that time was what he needed the most. When he did, his dad stepped up. Their bond grew deeper until his dad passed away.

But of course Andy's father has a legacy that lives on in his son. In their conversation about fathers in *Renegade: Born in the USA*, Bruce Springsteen and Barack Obama discuss the influence of fathers who have passed away. "Ancestors walk by your side and bring you comfort and a vision of life that will be yours,"

Springsteen reflects at one point. "My father walks beside me now like my ancestor. It took a long time for that to happen."

Andy's father's generosity lives on through Andy in his job as a fundraiser for people serving in ministry around the world. Whenever Andy is fishing, hunting, rooting for their favorite baseball team, or building something at home, the influence and legacy of his father continues.

Takeaways

Andy's story, like Joe's, is about presence. Andy's father offered presence emotionally through verbalizing "I love you," forehead kisses before heading out on long trips for work, and sharing in birthday conversations.

The type of presence Andy desired was for his father to be present for the things Andy placed value in, not because his father also enjoyed those activities but because they were important to Andy. This type of presence requires fathers to move out of loving in self-centered ways. It requires dads to expand into loving their children in ways that honor their children's interests and passions.

Andy's courage to have a tough conversation with his father—about how he was impacted by his dad's lack of presence—allowed his father to give voice to something that had been on his mind and heart. His courage opened up space for healing to take root.

This is a note to all fathers: It's possible that your children are waiting on you to acknowledge and give voice to what they, too, have been sitting with for some time. Andy's father provided further healing later in their relationship by taking the initiative to do the things Andy enjoyed, like fishing. This only deepens the connection between father and son.

Andy's father's commitment to ministry and the way it distracted him from being present with his family is a common story. It's the story of so many children of spiritual leaders. But the cultivation of family requires presence. A dysfunctional level of sacrificial service to an institution can be harmful. The first commitment of anyone in ministry or service is to their family.

Your emotional and spiritual presence as a father matters. Your children long to cultivate relationships and to embrace the things that you value. This is the sacred practice of your son knowing you and you knowing your son.

CONCLUSION

I learned so much from interviewing men about their "I Wish My Dad" stories. Each story I heard confirmed my original assumption: all of us—no matter how much money our families have or don't have, no matter where we live or how old we are or what culture we come from—need to experience love from our fathers in ways that allow us to feel emotionally safe. All of us desire deeper connections with our fathers. We want to be seen, valued, and treated like we matter more than work, money, or things. We want to hear the words "I love you." We want to be hugged by our dads. We want to know our fathers' stories: the challenges, fears, dreams, and childhood experiences that shaped who they became as men. We want to be seen for who we really are rather than who they want us to be. We want our dads to value and love who we are.

What do you walk away with as you reflect on these "I Wish My Dad" stories? Here are a few of the things I realized as I listened to men share their stories with me.

1. When we speak to our sons, even when they are young, we have to be mindful that our words have an impact on their future.
2. Our sons should be striving to become better and more loving men *because* of our example, not in spite of it.
3. We need to determine if we are passing down pain to our sons. Are we leaving the same emotional wounds in them that our dads left in us?

4. Maintaining a silence around our mistakes and trying to live as if they never happened, without ever addressing them, is not helpful.

5. Having hard but healing conversations with our sons means they may finally get the relationship they have always wanted to have with us. We as fathers and sons can both share in the reward.

Clinical psychologist Deryl Goldenberg expresses the goal of giving voice to our father-and-son stories this way:

> As men face the truth about their father–son bond, they will experience both pain and liberation. As they make their way through this emotional labyrinth, it can become a true "rite of passage." The son can emerge with a stronger sense of his identity and a solid sense of his own masculinity. The son can come to feel more integrated as a man and perhaps willing to see his father more realistically, with both positive and negative traits. Both father and son may be able to recognize more clearly how their negative unexpressed feelings may still be impacting their intimate relationships as well as intruding into their friendships with men.

Goldenberg suggests that one goal of coming to terms with our feelings about our dads is to "no longer be entangled with them through anger or hurt." He writes that men can carry "their newly earned individuation and energy into their love life, work life and friendships with other men." In short, emotional freedom that moves each of us along the journey toward wholeness is our hope.

As I listened to each man open up vulnerably and share his truth with me, I also felt convicted. That conviction was what compelled me to reach out to my son, Jordan, so that we could have our own hard yet healing conversation, which you'll find in the resources section.

I hope that if you are a father reading these stories, you will see all the ways in which you're getting it right. I hope, too, that if you also see the ways that you have been getting it wrong, you will push yourself to do things differently. I hope that you will be courageous enough to try. Break the cycle of toxic masculinity that has not served any of us well. Find ways to lay down your armor, hug your children, and tell them you love them. Spend time with them in ways that might make you uncomfortable but allow them to feel loved. Enter into their space on their terms, not yours.

I pray that you find healing where you need it and offer your children the opportunity to heal if they need it. I pray that you surrender to love and experience it fully so that you can offer it to others. There's a saying that "you only live once," but that's not true. You live every day, and you only die once. Use this one life to thrive, love, hug, cry, laugh, and be free.

I wish all of you a life well loved.

—Romal Tune

HOW TO HAVE YOUR OWN "I WISH MY DAD" CONVERSATION

Before you have an honest conversation with your son about his "I Wish My Dad" story, you will need to have an honest conversation with yourself. Reflect on the things you have done wrong, moments you missed, things you did not say and should have said. Own your mistakes and forgive yourself. Commit to being a better you and a better dad. Those two things are your "why."

Set aside ninety minutes to two hours for the interview. It may not take that long, but you want to make sure you have adequate time so that you are not interrupted or have to cut it short. When you sit down with your son, thank him for his willingness to have the conversation. Let him know you are aware it will not be easy for either of you, but it will be worth it. Make sure you're in a quiet place where you can't be interrupted and there are no distractions. Have some glasses of water and some tissues available, because one or both of you may cry during the process. If you do, remember that it's okay. If it happens, they will likely be healing tears.

It's very important to hold your son's answers with open hands. When you ask him to reflect on the "I Wish My Dad" questions, he needs to be able to speak freely and honestly without interruption. If you sense that he is holding back or trying to avoid certain topics and words to protect your feelings, let him know that it is okay. He can say what he needs to say. Ask probing but open-ended questions if you want him to expound on a statement. Don't ask questions that lead only to the kind of answers you want to hear.

You will likely hear him say things that you don't like. You might get uncomfortable, sad, or even angry. Remember that this is not about you—it's about him and healing. Whatever he says is likely something he has been holding on to for a long time, perhaps even years. Do not try to explain yourself or justify your behavior. Let him speak. If it is true, it's just true, even if it hurts. But this time, it will hurt for the last time and finally put you on a journey of healing. After all, healing is the goal.

Here are the three reflection statements to ask your son:

1. What comes to mind when you think about and reflect on the statement "When I think about love, I wish my dad..."?

2. What comes to mind when you think about and reflect on the statement "When I think about affection and things like being hugged, I wish my dad..."?

3. What comes to mind when you think about and reflect on the statement "When I think about time or quality time, I wish my dad..."?

Don't ask all three reflection questions at once. Ask the first one and let your son take the time he needs to respond. When he is done, ask if there is anything else he would like to share. If there is not, move to the next one and so on.

When the interview is over, thank your son for doing it. If necessary, apologize for specific things that he brought out, where you can clearly see he was hurting. Affirm how proud you are of him and tell him that you love him. If it feels uncomfortable or awkward to you, that's okay. It's new, but over time it will become second nature. Hugging and affirming your son should be normal, and it will begin to feel normal over time. You are breaking an old cycle that did not serve either of you well.

A lot of men I interviewed shared that they were tired after the interview. Some even decided to take the next day off from work to process their feelings. Self-care is very important after the process. If you need space and time, take it. You may want to talk to your therapist or a friend you can trust with your story. Tell them about the conversation, how you are feeling, what it was like to do it, and what you got from it. Sometimes it's helpful to have a listening ear.

You may also consider inviting your son to interview you about *your* dad. Many men, young and old, love hearing about their grandfathers. You may find that both of you learn some things in the process. It will give him a glimpse into your story and who you are and perhaps even allow you to see that some of the ways you built the relationship with your son were in fact connected to the relationship you had with your dad.

To give a very real sense of what this process is like, Jordan and I have included our "I Wish My Dad" conversations on the next few pages. In the first one, I interview Jordan about what he longed for but didn't always receive from me. In the second, Jordan interviews me about my relationship with my father. These pages have been only lightly edited for clarity, so they read a bit like a transcript. We thought it was important to give you this unfiltered version of our conversations. Vulnerable conversations between fathers and sons are powerful, and their power lies in their raw honesty and transparency. Receive these conversations from us as inspiration to have your own.

You may or may not be a Christian or person of faith. But after reading our interviews, which come next, you might wonder what would allow me to share such hard truths about myself in a book. It was because this passage of scripture kept coming to mind: "Therefore, there is now no condemnation for those who are in Christ Jesus" (Romans 8:1). I am not the man I once was. I forgive myself for my failures, and I pray that I am forgiven in return.

Jordan and I have shared our stories because we believe that if they can save someone's life or heal someone's sense of self or change someone's relationships for the better, then our vulnerability has been well worth it.

A FATHER-TO-SON CONVERSATION

ROMAL INTERVIEWS HIS SON
(JORDAN)

Romal: Jordan, I really am grateful you agreed to do this. Yes, it's bigger than any specific thing I could ever receive. So tell me: What kind of man am I? What kind of father?

Jordan: I guess, as a man, hardworking. I know that you came from and had a tough upbringing, which is something I'll have to pay attention to as I get older, and understand why certain things happened.

Romal: What do you mean by certain things?

Jordan: I guess environments are different because with me, you and my mother sheltered me, in a sense. I didn't have to grow up poor … and I know you did. I didn't see friends die. Even though my household was broken, there weren't different men and women running through the house … I also think you are compassionate but tough. You offer tough love. After ten years you left and went to Los Angeles, so I don't really know who you are entirely.

Romal: What don't you know about me?

Jordan: The man you are. When I turned sixteen, you didn't text me until that night. I cried. Things like that when you moved to L.A., I wouldn't see you until the summer. I didn't know if it was the work or because you didn't want to come back.

I was thinking I did something wrong. I am very introverted, and I don't really know how to show my emotions. I cry a lot, and I usually do that by myself. And after you said that Aman [Jordan's sister] and I always ask you for money, I tried to make sure I didn't ask for *anything*. It wasn't that I was ungrateful. I was absent-minded.

Romal: What did me living in Los Angeles do for our relationship?

Jordan: I thought the L.A. situation wasn't good for us and for you. I didn't recognize you when we went out to spend one summer. You were drinking Patrón a lot. We didn't like the woman in your life; she wasn't nice. It just seemed like you were always angry, making it a messy experience. All of it made us tense. One time with Aman, you yelled at her and she went in the bathroom and cried. It was a lot.

Romal: Do you have pleasant memories of me as a father?

Jordan: For a while I didn't like you. But I enjoyed when you came to my soccer games. That was a big thing for me. It was always good when you tried to push me in soccer, knowing that I could do better. Other than that, I don't have much more to reflect on because you and mom got divorced. I know the reasons why.

Me and Aman loved coming over for Christmas at your house—we lived in an apartment—because you would decorate, and that meant a lot to us. It showed that you cared. Overall, though, it is hard to say what you are because I didn't see you that much.

When I was five or six years old, we were in the bathroom, and you were doing Aman's hair. You made a promise: that you and mom would never get divorced. I never forgot that. Then for it to happen and *why* it happened … I was just angry.

Romal: Why did it happen?

Jordan: You cheated. And you put your hands on my mom. I don't know the full details of everything, but I know those are some of the reasons.

Romal: What did you think of me?

Jordan: I basically forced my mom to tell me. I was yelling at her and she ended up blurting it out by accident. I was angry. I was shocked because I wanted to be like you so much, and then finding out stuff like that changed my perspective a little bit.

Romal: How did that perspective change?

Jordan: I grew up quickly. I knew I couldn't be like you. And that was tough. I would still go to school and glorify you to all my friends, but I would get angry and would have to watch myself.

Romal: You said there was a time when you wanted to be like me and then you didn't. What were the things you wanted to be like, and what were the things you did not want to be like?

Jordan: I think every son wants to be like his father. I looked at someone who was bigger than me and smarter than me. I saw you work. I saw us move from one house to a bigger house and from an apartment to a big house. I thought if I could be as successful as you...

At the time, I used to think I could follow your career path as a legacy thing, but it's not really my passion. I love to help people. I just wanted to take a different path because law is so beautiful to me. As for what I didn't want to be like related to you, I don't want to have a broken household. I don't want to get divorced.

Romal: How do you think about love and the phrase "I wish my dad..."?

Jordan: I wish you were there more. I wish there were moments when you didn't give tough love. Sometimes when you said certain things, you might not have meant to come off as tough love, but to me it sounded like that.

Romal: In what kinds of things?

Jordan: If I didn't do well in a game, you would be like, "Why am I doing this or that?" Growing up, we all make mistakes. It was the instant tough love approach—angry and sudden—instead of explaining it in a nice way. I didn't need that with every situation. Certain situations didn't have to be so aggressive.

Romal: What would love have looked like in the way you needed it?

Jordan: You would have to look at the framework of my mother. For me, a better answer is that love is simply being there. My mom was there for everything. That is why she is my best friend. Her love has always been there, and she's always being encouraging.

The tough love is really bad. In middle school, I got a 2.8 grade point average after my grandfather died, and she gave me a talk and she said just do better. I got a 3.5 GPA the rest of the year. It is motivation and remembering that you can do better because someone tells you that you can do better every day. At Morehouse, I have a 3.4 GPA. It wasn't a great start, but I got the support I needed from mom, not you.

My senior year when you had a business trip in Virginia, you drove an hour to my school. That meant a lot because you went out of your way and you came to my f*cking school. You didn't know if I had class or anything, you just came. I was able to see you, and that meant a lot. It meant a lot because I never saw you. My mom would drop something off and leave. I wish I could have grown up with that from you too.

Romal: When you think about affection, you wish I …

Jordan: I am not an affectionate person. With my girlfriend, I've learned how to talk to someone every day and not hate it. I've learned that I can be affectionate and show my emotions to someone who is not my best friend Rob, who I told everything. I don't know if that is because of you or just because of how I was born. When I was younger, you used to put your head on my head and just play. That was good for me. When we would watch movies until 3 a.m., that was enough for me. I didn't really feel like there was so much affection I missed, because I don't like people touching me a lot. I'm not saying affection has to be touching. I don't need phone calls for affection. I just need quality time. You've got to be there.

Romal: What do you feel when you consider words of affirmation like "I love you?"

Jordan: I think because we both grew up in a one-parent household, I feel like affection is kind of lost—not lost, but I don't look for it. When you did say, "I love you," it was enough for me. When I got good grades, you said, "Good job." When you sat with me on the phone after my mentor, Willie J. Lovett, died and just talked to me, that was enough affection for me. That really isn't what I was missing. It's the lost opportunities for quality time throughout my childhood that hurt.

Romal: You have a number of experiences when you say the time we did spend "was not great." But it sounds like you would prefer those cases over me not being there.

Jordan: I think sometimes it really wasn't your fault because it was at a point when I was young, when I hated you for the divorce and for the reasons of the divorce and not understanding why everything happened so quickly. Why did I have to leave this big house, a school with all of my friends? I had all those thoughts in my head. Sometimes you could do the littlest thing and I was like *I want to go home* because I already had this thought in my head about the person you were.

I thought you were a bad person, and I didn't forget things. When I was six or seven, you told me you didn't like your father because he put his hands on your mother. So I had that same idea about that issue because you had it. But then you put my mother through the same thing, so I didn't like you.

Romal: So there was this conflict you battled: You wanted me around, but you were angry with me.

Jordan: Yes. The trips to L.A. to visit you weren't the best. We would do some cool things, but then the people around you were not cool.

Romal: My biggest two regrets are not being there for my kids and leaving. I used to justify why I left—*Oh, I need to go make some money* or *Oh, I just hate DC*. I didn't hate DC; I hated who I was. Growing up, I was always moving and always leaving something. I didn't know how to stay and fight for anyone. I was not a good person. I had terrible character that resulted in an affair.

I didn't have solid values. I was selfish. My ego was toxic. It drove my behavior and disconnected me from you guys. As for your mother, I won't even call it a fight, because it wasn't.

Your mom and I were trying to work things out after the affair. Several years later, my mom was diagnosed with terminal lung cancer. I decided that she would move in with us. I went to California to bring her to DC. The night that I got there, she was put on life support, something she and I had discussed. She had said, "If that ever happens, let my brothers and my sister come see me and then take me off." I did everything she asked. Then she died the next day.

I buried her three days later. I was depressed. I wouldn't leave the house. I would lie on the couch and sleep. I was angry. I was distant.

One day, your mom wanted us to go to dinner with some of her friends who were moving to Texas. I didn't want to go, sparking an argument:

"You're just like your mom," she said.

"Don't talk about my mom."

"My mom was there for you when your mom was f*cking dying," she said.

I jumped out of the bed, and I grabbed her. I don't know how it happened, but I had a cut on my neck. I think when she was trying to make me let her go, the glass broke and I got cut.

Jordan: Yes, I know. We were standing outside the door.

Romal: I pushed her head down on the bed. I grabbed her by the neck, and when I did that, I knew it was over. That's when I realized, *We're done, because this is not who I am. I just ruined everything. I just went against everything I am.* I let her up and said, "You got to go."

That was the culmination of years of my bullshit. The depression from my mom dying and the argument led to that moment, and I wish I had it back. I have played that scenario over and over in my head. *I could have done things so differently. That didn't have to happen.*

Then you all were gone. You had moved out.

I sat on the kitchen floor one night and contemplated suicide. I tried to figure out how I was going to do it ... and I prayed. Then I called the suicide hotline. That triggered me out of it, ironically, because they put me on hold, and I was pissed. How do you put a caller to a suicide hotline on hold?

I prayed again. "God, you have got to show me some people in the Bible like me." That led to me writing the book *God's Graffiti.*

That is why I wanted to have this conversation with you. My father has never admitted his wrongs, has never apologized. I need you to know that I am aware of the pain I have caused you and I am so sorry.

You are already a better man than I was at your age. You are an introvert like me. You keep a small circle. In listening to you, I can tell we are a lot alike. You would have known that before now, if I had been there.

Jordan: I was scared that I was just like you. I haven't cheated on anyone, but I have helped someone cheat. I have terrible anger issues. I have cried about it with so many people. It seems like it's a cycle in our family: from grandfather to you to me. That I'm going to end up doing some bad shit is my biggest fear. I have pushed people away because of it. I have f*cked up so many good relationships like you have simply out of the fear of not understanding how to be in a relationship. My mom showed me love, but every time I tried to do the same, I would think of bad things that could happen. I didn't want to get to a point where it would get messed up, so I would just end it and I would do it in the worst ways. I would start an argument with someone.

One of my closest friends, we don't talk anymore. She was literally my everything as a friend, everything I needed in a friend, and I f*cked it up because I was scared she was breaking away, so I ended it so I could say I did it. Even though that situation of what you did pissed me off, I can see myself doing it.

We are so much alike, according to my mom. You and my mom might not have a relationship, but she never talked bad on your name. Ever.

Romal: It takes time and work to get past pushing people away. It's called abandonment issues. Yours are tied to me not being there.

Jordan: That shit makes me so f*cking angry and it is frustrating because I don't know how to fix it. At times I know I am doing it, but I just can't stop it.

Romal: What we are doing right now is a part of fixing it.

Jordan: You brought up the issue of ego. Mine has skyrocketed. Only God knows why. I always check this Muhammad Ali quote, "To be the greatest you have to believe you are the greatest." My ego is like that.

Romal: But a part of ego is tied to me not being there and creating that abandonment issue. *If I were enough, my dad wouldn't have left.*

Jordan: I never blamed myself for you leaving. But I think I definitely have issues of abandonment. It stems from—not saying you're wrong—going to school with a bunch of white people. In the advanced placement classes, they would always treat me like I was dumb. My ego grew because I didn't want them to think I was dumb. But I feel like abandonment can add to the ego. I'm still going through it. Everyone at Morehouse has a huge ego, and I feel like I have more to prove. Sometimes I'm like: *I can't get a bad grade because if you see it, you would not be happy.*

Romal: When you were little, you used to have insane test anxiety. It was this fear of not getting a good grade and me being mad at or disappointed in you. I told you: *I love you and it is a constant. It is not "I love you because…" I love you. You are my son.*

Jordan: You have to remember, though, I saw how successful you were. Now I want to be at a point where I can make a substantial living. I want to be at your success level, but even higher just to also prove myself. But also, I can't struggle again.

Romal: Jordan, I get that, but the greatest success you're going to ever have is becoming a better you and living into who you are meant to be. Attainment of stuff and money and homes isn't true success. Being a person of good character and values, living at the highest caliber of human being you can become: that is real success.

I used to sleep in a closet. My greatest fear is being homeless again. But the motivating factor for me is taking every gift that God has given me and using it to the good of other people.

In reflecting on your own "I Wish My Dad" story, can you relate to this interview? If so, how?

Do you have your own takeaways or lessons learned? If so, what are they?

A SON-TO-FATHER CONVERSATION

JORDAN INTERVIEWS HIS DAD
(ROMAL)

Jordan: What kind of man was your dad?

Romal: My dad worked hard. I met my dad when I was fifteen years old. When I was in about the fifth grade, my mom told me he had died in a car accident. She didn't want me to have a relationship with him. She held a lot of anger toward him, which I later learned wasn't his fault. I think a lot of it was around her wanting him to send money. There was a time when she wanted him to send more and he wanted a relationship with me and she would use me to punish him and never let him speak to me. A lot of things were tied to that. I grew up for a long time thinking he was dead.

While I was in junior high, one day I was home from school, I think maybe eighth grade, and the phone rang. On the other end was a man with a deep, unfamiliar voice. The conversation went something like this: "Hi Romal, can I speak to your mom?"

I told him she wasn't home and he said, "Do you know who this is?"

I replied, "No."

"I'm Gary. I'm your father."

I said, "My dad is dead." He said, "No, I'm your dad. Your mom hasn't told you about me?"

I said, "No."

He said, "How are you doing?"

I got off the phone with him and my mom got home that day and I told her a man named Gary called. "He said he was my dad." She got upset and that is when I knew it was true. She said, "What is he doing calling here? What did he say?"

I thought, *Oh, my God. That was my father.*

We still never had a relationship. We talked on the phone. He lived in New Jersey.

After that day, we would talk occasionally over the phone. When I was fifteen, my mom finally let me go see him in New Jersey. I spent the summer and had a great time. We went to eat when he picked me up from the airport. He was nervous and I felt awkward, but that summer turned out great. We went to theme parks and he bought me all kinds of stuff. But he drank and smoked cigarettes a lot. Still, it was fun. After about a month, I went home.

About a year later, some things happened in my life and I wanted to get away from California. I called him and asked if I could come stay with him. He said yes, so I moved to New Jersey. I lived with him for two years and finished out eleventh and twelfth grade. Those two years weren't like the summer I enjoyed. It was hell.

A bit of background about my dad: his own parents had died when he was around five. His mom died from an asthma attack, and his father died a year or so later from a brain tumor. An aunt raised him in Newark, New Jersey. When he was only seventeen, my dad lied about his age and entered the marine corps. He went to Vietnam in a demolitions unit, and his job was to crawl into tunnels to see if there were explosives. I'm certain a lot of stress came with a job that put him in position to be blown up. He saw a lot of death and violence in Vietnam. So he had a challenging childhood, followed by an equally traumatic military stint.

When I lived with him during those last days of high school, he was drinking daily. He was physically fit, and he would always lift weights at home. He kept dumbbells in his bedroom. He was also angry every day. He was mean. He would come home from work and more often than not, he would yell at my brothers and curse at me. I was lazy. I was stupid. I wasn't going to amount to anything. He would go in the kitchen, pour himself a drink, heat up his food, and retreat to his room, and we wouldn't see him for the rest of the night. That was every day. There was fear of what might happen when he came home. He got physical with me once, but he regularly threatened and berated me, which made me feel like crap all the time. I was the oldest of his four boys that included Corey, Shannon, and Jason.

My dad didn't spend a lot of time with us; instead he loaded us up with a lot of chores. It was always: "Go cut the grass," or "Clean this," or "Wash the dishes," or "Do the laundry," and that was it. The one time he got physical with me was when I drove his car without permission. A cousin was in town, and we went riding around. When I got home, he grabbed me and threw me up against the wall. He said, "If you ever take my car again, I'm going to kill you." He scared the shit out of me.

I was a much better athlete than student. Running track, I could have gotten a scholarship, but I didn't have the grades. With graduation approaching, my dad told me: "The day you graduate, we're done. You can't come back to my house so you'll have to find somewhere to go. You can't come back."

So literally after the graduation ceremony and the good-byes, I put all my stuff into a friend's car. I had nowhere to go. I lived on the streets or with friends for a few weeks, sleeping in an alley once. And then I joined the army.

So you ask, what kind of man was my dad? He was hardworking. He was a disciplinarian. He was mean. He was a harsh man. And he drank a lot.

Jordan: What kind of father is your dad?

Romal: He didn't spend time with us at all. We never did anything together. We never played any sports together or sat down to have any man-to-man time. He never taught me anything about life or what it was to be a man; he just told me what I wasn't and what I couldn't be instead. As a father, he was a provider. He had a nice home in New Jersey. He was able to pay bills and put food on the table. It's funny because now that we have reconnected in recent years, I call him "Pop." I don't call him "Dad." I don't feel like I have that kind of relationship. I feel like "Dad" has a different kind of intimacy. The way I grew up, you call older people "Pop." You feel affection for them, but it is not the intimate connection of a dad. My dad and I never had that bond.

Jordan: How did that make you feel?

Romal: For years I hated him—and I mean hated him. I hated him because of all that my mom went through. I felt like he wasn't supportive of her, which I later learned was not true. I hated the way he talked about her; he would always point out her addictions. But my thing was always, "She didn't leave; you did." I later learned the dynamics leading up to why he left. He hadn't wanted to leave. He had actually wanted to stay and be a family, but she hadn't. I was angry that he wasn't there for me. I was angry that when I did meet him and lived with him, it didn't meet my expectations. It was a terrible experience.

I grew up in the inner city and learned life on the streets from my well-known uncles who dominated them. So the nice dad I had in my head—who played sports, had endless fun, and was going to teach me about life—did not exist. He simply wasn't equipped to be that.

My literary agent, Adrienne Ingrum, said to me once, "You still sound angry with your dad and don't show him any grace or forgiveness. Given the challenges you have had with your children, one day you are going to want grace and forgiveness from them. So you need to offer that to your dad, because you are going to want and need it one day."

She was right. I was not present for my kids. I was hopeful that one day I would be offered grace and forgiveness, and I realized that I needed to offer my father the same.

Jordan: So now you and I have gotten to a place where I am able to forgive you and understand. Have you been able to get there with your father? Have you been able to see him, forgive him?

Romal: I have been able to forgive him, and here is why: Two years ago, I went to see him for the first time in thirteen years. I had not seen him since my mom passed away. I remember wanting to be angry but knew I needed to deal with it head-on in order to overcome it. I was thinking about all the old grievances and wondered if he would ever admit to owning how poorly he treated me or maybe even say, "I'm sorry." I wasn't optimistic. My friend Rudy told me, "Your dad is seventy-three years old. He is in the last quarter of his life. You have done a lot of work on yourself to heal. He may never be able to give you what you need. But because of the man you are—because of the inner emotional work you've done—you can give him what he needs even if he can never give you what you need."

I didn't like hearing that from Rudy, but he was right. So when I reconnected with my dad, I didn't show up as a wounded, angry child. I showed up as a man. We had a good conversation. I learned some things about his story and about his family that I didn't know. He shared what little he knew about my grandparents, making my visit feel less awkward and more informative. Then I saw him again three months later and my three stepbrothers and I reunited. It was the first time in over thirty years that all four of us were under the same roof... and it, too, went well.

A short time later I went to see him. We just hung out and talked. I asked questions and we even hugged when it was time to leave, so we are definitely on a better path.

Jordan: When you think about love, how would you complete the sentence: "I wish my dad..."?

Romal: I wish my dad treated me like he loved me. I wish he had talked to me like he loved me. Even though I got in trouble or I wasn't working hard, I wish that he would have spoken life to me and disciplined me in a manner to where I didn't feel inadequate. I wish he would have encouraged or inspired me to do better. I felt if he loved me the way I needed to be loved, he would have treated me differently or talked to me like he loved me.

He never said "I love you" when I was growing up, and I am grateful he's able to say it now. That phrase was absent when I was growing up and I always questioned if he really cared.

Jordan: Do you think that you acted out because you weren't getting love from your father, at least the love you wanted?

Romal: Yes, maybe in some ways I was lashing out because of all I had been through without the presence of a father figure. But I also grew up in an environment where people just taught you how to survive; they didn't teach you how to feel. In my family, no one really talked about love. Although my grandfather would say he loved me from time to time, my grandmother didn't say it. She did show love through her actions, expressing it in the way she talked to me. I was the same kid with them that I was with my father, but they would look beyond my behavior to see who I could become. That's what I wanted from him. I wanted to succeed and to prove my dad wrong. My strong desire for success stemmed from resentment for him. For my grandparents, it was out of love. I wanted them to see they were right about me.

Jordan: So when you think about affection, how would you finish the sentence: "I wish my dad …"?

Romal: When I think about affection, I wish my dad would have shown me that I don't have to be hard all the time and I wish he would have hugged me and told me he loved me. I wish he would have treated me more gently rather than being harsh all the time.

I wish he would have shown me that there are times when you need to be a warrior and there are times when you need to put the armor down and just be human. There are times to admit when you are sad or when you are afraid. I wish he would have just let me know I was going to be okay.

Jordan: Like a guide, almost?

Romal: Yes, like a guide, showing me how to be a healthy man and how to have feelings and to know that crying or being sad doesn't make you less of man.

Jordan: Finally: "When I think about quality time, I wish my dad …"

Romal: I wish we would have gone bike riding together. He had a garden in the back, and my grandfather had a garden. My grandfather used to show me how to plow and till soil, and all the ins and outs of gardening and growing your own food. I wish my dad had done that with me, other than just telling me to go pick up the trash. I wish we could have hung out and talked about life and that he would have shared his journey and his story with me.

I wish we had played sports together; I loved sports growing up. I ran track, and he never came to a single meet. One time we were headed to state finals and the night before my team and I went out to celebrate. We were drinking at someone's house, and I got drunk and fell and broke my hand. They took me to the emergency room. We had the cross-country state finals in the morning, and I wanted to run. The doctor said I shouldn't, but he said he could put an air cast on it and I could run if I had permission from my dad. He called my dad, who said: "Well, if you're stupid enough to still run..."

That's how he gave permission. I ran and I did well. I was on the front page of the sports section. My dad didn't care. So I wish he had been a part of those things and shown up and supported me or at least told me how proud he was of how good of a job I was doing or something.

Jordan: How do you feel your dad's relationship with you affected you with your kids?

Romal: He didn't prepare me for being a dad. Maybe, if anything, it was about provision not about presence. I was very superficial and cared way too much about how my kids looked, what they were wearing, and my next money move. I convinced myself that it was about them because, after all, my kids had plenty of stuff. But that was all rooted in my being selfish and finding a reason to justify it. I later realized that I had it all wrong. Just like I wanted my dad, my kids wanted my time and attention, and no material item could replace that.

The way I was brought up had me believing that life was about success and money. I later learned that parenting has nothing to do with any of that. Parenting is about love and affection and time spent together and pouring into your children in a way that makes them become better than you.

It's about seeing who they can become and doing whatever it takes to make sure they become their best selves. It's about letting them know how proud you are of them, how much you love and believe in them. And that doesn't cost anything.

Jordan: There were times after you and my mom got divorced that you kept buying us stuff. Even as a kid, I always knew that was just a way of covering up what you couldn't do more as a parent. Hearing you say it now is almost a relief, because I see that you've learned and obviously are attempting to do better. But if you can be honest with yourself, would you say there is still resentment you have for your father?

Romal: I don't think so. I don't have any resentment toward him, because I get it now. It doesn't replace or negate what did or didn't happen. Holding him accountable to the past would only make me miss the present. I am not an angry kid anymore, and he's not the mean drill sergeant anymore. I see him as a man I love from who I am not and not who I was.

I understand how important love, affection, and time are now. That is why I am always asking you when you are coming over so we can hang out. I appreciate that time now.

Jordan: By the grace of God, I was gifted with a bunch of father figures growing up; even my mom was a father figure. I had my best friend, Jacob, whose dad treated me like his kid. Theo's father treated me like I was his own. That helped bring out the resentment. But I am grateful I am able to learn about you and that you can learn about me now, and not when I am forty or fifty years old. You missed the childhood but, mind you, I still have an entire adulthood to go.

Romal: To hear you say that you had father figures still knocks the wind out of me. It hurts. But you're right: God has definitely used these interviews for you and me as a tool to have some conversations that we needed to have.

Jordan: I thank you for this conversation and not judging how I felt. This is like a new chapter has begun. It really is healing. I can move on in my relationship with my father.

Romal: I earned that anger that you had. I needed to hear it so you didn't carry it with you.

Jordan: I knew someday this would come out—and for it to happen a lot sooner than I thought it would will generally help me move on with life. And it helps you move on as well.

I enjoyed how I said it, and I didn't hate saying it. But I felt like you were actually listening. I thought a lot of those feelings I felt over time had diminished, but they were still there. And being able to understand why I act a certain way around the idea of abandonment and why I push so many people away. This new understanding—it has already helped me.

I am proud of who I am becoming, though I still have a lot of work to do.

In reflecting on your own "I Wish My Dad" story, can you relate to this interview? If so, how?

Do you have your own takeaways or lessons learned? If so, what are they?

ACKNOWLEDGMENTS

Thank you to all of the men featured in this book for your courage, transparency, and authenticity. Your stories will give other men permission to speak their truth and, God willing, experience healing. Thanks to:

Jorge Acevedo

Ernest Brooks

Joseph W. Daniels, Jr.

Kamasi Hill

Philip L. Hillman

Andy Ivey

Robert E. Lee

Michael-Ray Mathews

Daniel (pseudonym)

Rudy Rasmus

Kevin Robert

Vance P. Ross

Simon (pseudonym)

Isaac Sparks

Max Wilkens

Hodari Williams

Andre C. Young

Thank you to Kendra Frazier, licensed therapist, for writing the takeaways for each chapter. Your wisdom provides critical insights for readers.

To my father, Gary Tune: I still wish we had the relationship that I always wanted. Sometimes I'm still saddened by the thoughts of a father and son connection between us that didn't exist when I was a kid. I love you, Dad, and I know you love me too. I'm grateful that there's still time for us to get better at loving each other the way that we need it. To my son Jordan: I am so proud of you. I am grateful for the healing that began because of the interview between you and me. As we continue to heal, our relationship will become even healthier. I love you, son, and my only desire is for you to be free from the limitations of unhealed trauma so that you can thrive.

NOTES

3 "Fatherly Figures: A Snapshot of Dads Today," United States Census Bureau, June 12, 2018, https://www.census.gov/library/visualizations/2018/comm/fathers-day.html.

52 Eric D. Miller, "Why the Father Wound Matters: Consequences for Male Mental Health and the Father-Son Relationship," *Child Abuse Review* 22(3): 195.

105 W. E. B. Du Bois, *The Souls of Black Folk: Essays and Sketches* (Chicago: A. G. McClurg, 1903), 2.

127 Ta-Nehisi Coates, *The Beautiful Struggle: A Father, Two Sons, and an Unlikely Road to Manhood* (New York: Spiegel & Grau, 2008), 206.

150 Barack Obama and Bruce Springsteen, *Renegades: Born in the USA* (New York: Crown, 2021), condensed and excerpted in "Springsteen and Obama on Friendship and Fathers," *Guardian*, October 23, 2021, https://www.theguardian.com/culture/2021/oct/23/bruce-springsteen-and-barack-obama-on-friendship-and-fathers-book-renegades.

199 *Ibid.*

204 Deryl Goldenberg, "The Psychology Behind Strained Father Son Relationships," *PsychAlive*, accessed November 12, 2021, https://www.psychalive.org/psychology-behind-strained-father-son-relationships/.